Prayers
OF COMFORT & HOPE

HOLDING ON TO FAITH

Publications International, Ltd.

Christine A. Dallman is a freelance writer living near Everett, Washington. She is the author of *Daily Devotions for Seniors*, an inspirational resource for maturing adults, as well as coauthor of several other Publications International, Ltd., titles.

Louis Weber, CEO
Publications International, Ltd.
7373 North Cicero Avenue
Lincolnwood, Illinois 60712

Permission is never granted for commercial purposes.

ISBN-13: 978-1-4508-7089-4
ISBN-10: 1-4508-7089-9

Manufactured in China.

8 7 6 5 4 3 2 1

Library of Congress Control Number: 2013946552

Table of Contents

Talking with God

*U*nto You I lift up my eyes,
O You who dwell in the heavens.

—Psalm 123:1

*G*od's Word reminds us to turn to the Lord
in all times: in times of joy and times of trial.
Sometimes, when we are distressed or worried,
we can find it difficult to express our thoughts
in prayer, even as we know we will find strength,
consolation, and renewed faith in talking and
listening to our Creator. *Prayers of Comfort and Hope*
is intended as a tool to help you draw more deeply
into a dialogue with God.

*T*he book is composed of ten chapters, each
chapter dealing with common hardships and
obstacles that threaten to separate us from
fellowship with God and others. The prayers,

scripture verses, and inspirational quotes found in each chapter are meant to give you ways of addressing these burdens as you confront them in your own life. You'll find prayers written from the heart by people like you, prayers of petition and praise, lamentation and thanksgiving, uncertainty and confident hope.

To use the book, set aside some time and find a quiet, restful place where you can sit in stillness with the Lord. Sift through a chapter that meets your needs and find the prayer or prayers that speak to your situation. Read and reflect, and then take some time to let the words sink in. Maybe the prayer on the page will help you formulate your own words. Maybe you'll want to contemplate what you've read in silence as you wait for God's insight.

The Lord turn his face toward you
and give you peace
—Numbers 6:26, NIV

CHAPTER 1

Coping with Depression and Disappointment

Answer me speedily, O Lord;
My spirit fails! Do not hide Your face
from me . . . . Cause me to hear
Your lovingkindness in the morning,
For in You do I trust; Cause me to know
the way in which I should walk,
For I lift up my soul to You.

—Psalm 143:7–8

A deepening gloom has engulfed my soul, Lord.
I hear some say that real people of faith don't
struggle with dark feelings and bad moods. But
when I look at the Psalms, I can hear in the
writers' voices what at times sounds exactly like
depression—the same kinds of thoughts and
feelings I struggle with. So here is my request:
I need to be able to come to you without fear
that you will be upset with me for where I'm at
in heart and mind right now. I'm willing to be
helped. I just need to feel safe approaching you
as I am. Thank you for listening, for caring about
what concerns me, and most of all for loving me
at all times.

*H*ear my prayer, O Lord,
And let my cry come to You . . . .
For my days are consumed like smoke,
And my bones are burned like a hearth.
My heart is stricken and withered like grass,
So that I forget to eat my bread.
—Psalm 102:1, 3–4

Father, I realize now that even people of faith have different struggles with discouragement and depression. It's a relief to realize that I'm not the only one. But where do I go from here? I need your wisdom and guidance. I guess this time of prayer is the best place to begin. Just being reminded that you are near keeps me from the despair of feeling all alone, and it's comforting to feel so heard and understood when I'm talking with you. I need you to help me through this day, Father. Just this day. I'll take them one at a time with you.

The Christian life is not a constant high.
I have my moments of deep discouragement.
I have to go to God in prayer with tears in my eyes,
and say, "O God, forgive me," or "Help me."
—Billy Graham

It feels as though I'm stuck, Lord. It seems like I've been waiting and praying and hoping to no avail. Please tell me what I am supposed to do. I long to see my way clearly to doing *something*— something that would lead me to the fresh air of improved circumstances. So I'm asking you to lead me to action if there is action I need to take. But, Lord, if I am supposed to keep waiting, I need encouragement and hope. You're the only one who can truly lift my spirit by your Spirit of patience, peace, and hope. Thank you for staying with me through this. I don't know what I would do without you.

Comfort, comfort ye my people,
Speak ye peace, thus saith our God;
Comfort those who sit in darkness,
Mourning 'neath their sorrows' load.
—Johann Olearius, translated Catherine Winkworth,
"Comfort, Comfort Ye My People"

Come to Me, all *you* who labor and are
heavy laden, and I will give you rest.

—Matthew 11:28

I didn't imagine that marriage would be so
difficult, Father. In my naiveté, I hoped it would
be more like something out of a movie script. I'm
all too aware now that real life is nothing like the

movies. For one thing, married life is definitely not scripted. And for another, there are a lot of mundane scenes between the highlights. Now I understand what people tried to tell me: Being married is a lot of hard work. Good relationships don't just happen; they're like a field that needs plowing and planting and watering and weeding. Oh, Father! I need your help! I want my marriage to stay alive and thrive. Please bring us back to the kind of mutual love and respect that is the basis for every good relationship. Help me focus on my part as I quietly pray for us both.

Some believe that the best of love
is always at its budding, but it is the full
bloom of an autumn rose that is most
fragrant and glorious.

*A*nother tragic event in our nation, Father! I look at the world and wonder what is going to become of us. I wonder if this will ever be a world where children can enjoy a carefree existence as they once did. I wonder where the kind of innocence I enjoyed as a child has gone. And I wonder what the world will look like in another twenty years. But even now, you remind me that life in this world does not last forever. In fact, even the longest lived person has had but a brief sojourn here when compared with the eternal life you hold out for those who put their trust in you. Thank you for the promise of life with you beyond this one, a life where darkness will not touch even the edges of our existence.

In our sad condition our only consolation
is the expectancy of another life.
—Martin Luther

Casting all your care upon Him,
for He cares for you.

—1 Peter 5:7

Today, Lord, I am weary of fighting the good fight of faith. I wonder if my efforts are of any consequence or any benefit to anyone. I said this out loud recently to someone you have put in my life—someone who has been through her own dark time. She gently counseled me to "keep on doing the next right thing." The benefits, she says, may be down the road, but if I choose the high road no matter what, I'll never have to endure regret. I know that's true, Lord. In my discouragement and disappointment, help me not give up, and please give me the strength and insight today to do that next right thing.

Any man can work when every stroke of his hands brings down the fruit rattling from the tree to the ground but to labor in season and out of season, under every discouragement . . . that requires a heroism which is transcendent.

—Henry Ward Beecher

*H*eavenly Father, I confess to you that I have not always made good and right choices along my way. Many times I have known what was right and yet have done my "own thing." Living with the consequences of such decisions brings me sorrow, not because I think it should have turned out differently, but because I know you had my best interest at heart all along, and I didn't trust you enough to listen and follow your lead. But I'm so grateful that you've never cast me aside. The truth is, you always lift me up when I come back to you, and you help me get through. Your lovingkindness and faithfulness have taught me how trustworthy you really are—that when you say no or tell me to wait, you are really keeping me from harm. Not only that, but you're also preparing only the best things for me.

*R*evive me, O Lord, for Your name's sake!
For Your righteousness' sake bring
my soul out of trouble.

—Psalm 143:11

We speak so casually of death sometimes. But, oh Lord! It is standing right in front of me now. I cannot avoid the shadow it casts over my whole being. There is nothing casual about this reality. It is a stark, unrelenting actuality that has entered my life. I don't want to open my eyes in the morning and come back to face it. Oh, God! Please, make it go away! How am I supposed to do this? How am I supposed to keep going? Please help me. Please hold me. I need you to just be with me right now and whisper your comfort and care. Then later, when I am ready to hear it, remind me of the hope that is eternal life in you.

The most comforting lullaby is the sound of God's tender heart beating for his children: "Come to me," it bids, "and you will find rest for your souls."

Oh, Savior! You find me here in the midst of a terrible funk. And I admit I haven't been doing much to fight it. Why do I avoid the very things that can help me most when I'm discouraged? I've not been connecting with the people I know are looking out for me. I haven't been going to my usual weekly gatherings where I find truth and encouragement. I look at my Bible sitting there, knowing I can find help and hope in its pages, but I just don't pick it up. In the Psalms it says that your Word is a lamp to my feet, a light to my path. I know I need your light to shine in this dark place, so I'll take this one small step today: I will read a passage, maybe a psalm, as you begin walking me back into the light.

Trust in the Lord with all your heart,
And lean not on your own
understanding; In all your ways
acknowledge Him, And He shall
direct your paths.

—Proverbs 3:5–6

*The remedy for discouragement is the
Word of God. When you feed your heart and
mind with its truth, you regain your
perspective and find renewed strength.*
—Warren Wiersbe

$\mathscr{L}$et down again! I'm so tired of this, Father. I get my hopes up, but the promises have come up empty once again. I try to give the benefit of the doubt, to trust the sincerity I see and hear, to believe something is really going to change. But it never does. What do I need to do? I don't want to walk away. But I do want things to change. I can't live like this—going from disappointment to disappointment. A friend recommended a book about boundaries. I'm not sure what that's all about, but maybe it's worth looking into. Please guide me into what living in truth and love looks like in this relationship, and grant me the courage to walk in it. Thank you for holding me up and for always being faithful to me. You're the one I know I can count on.

*Sometimes love has to speak up for truth,
and sometimes truth has to speak up for love.
They are fraternal twins, inseparable,
always defending one another.*

Every time I get ready to go to work, Lord, I wonder if I can endure another day of it. Please don't get me wrong; I'm thankful to have an income. I truly am. I know that to be jobless right now would be devastating. But the atmosphere at work is depressing. Leaders are making decisions that undermine morale. Coworkers are turning against one another in a culture of blame and unhealthy competition. I try to just "fly under the radar" and do my job, but I feel a sense of impending doom . . . like it's all going to fall apart. Please shelter me from the dysfunction, and help me maintain my integrity. I need your wisdom for getting through the day and also for knowing whether I should stay or look elsewhere. Thank you, Lord.

When life seems like a minefield,
there is no one I'd rather have leading me
than the one who sees and knows where
I can safely place my feet at every step.

*A*nd do not be conformed to this world,
but be transformed by the renewing of your
mind, that you may prove what *is* that good
and acceptable and perfect will of God.

—Romans 12:2

$\mathcal{B}$ut You, O Lord, *are* a shield for me,
My glory and the One who lifts up my head.
—Psalm 3:3

$\mathcal{W}$hen things are going well and I'm up, I feel like I'll never be low again. But here I am, heavenly Father, sent sprawling once again by intense feelings of shame because of a failure. I know other people may think it's a small thing and I should just get over it, but it seems like a big thing to me. You know me well, how even my small mistakes can feel like epic incompetence. Well, I realize I have a choice here. I can be derailed for days by this, or I can come to you for help to find perspective and self-forgiveness and let this be a short-lived disappointment. I know feeling down is part of being human, but I don't want to be characterized by it. So I'm going to choose to listen to you. Thank you, Father, for your Spirit of truth to encourage my heart.

Fits of depression come over the most of us.
Usually cheerful as we may be,
we must at intervals be cast down.
The strong are not always vigorous,
the wise not always ready,
the brave not always courageous,
and the joyous not always happy.
—Charles H. Spurgeon, "When a Preacher Is Downcast"

$\mathcal{I}$ think I lost a friendship, Father. My perspective on a particular matter is a deal breaker for my friend. I feel so disappointed. I thought our relationship could transcend any difference we might have. In fact, I can't believe this has happened. I truly value this person. Lord, you know I didn't try to force my viewpoint. But when the topic came up, I thought it was safe to express myself. Is there a way to restore the relationship? Or should I let it go? Please show me if my attitude was not right, or if something I said was out of line. I'd be glad to make amends if there are any I need to make. But if this is truly the end of our friendship, help me not become bitter but to love regardless of whether I am loved in return.

Rejection is one of the greatest disappointments we face on earth, but God's acceptance of us is the greatest balm for that pain.

If one more thing goes wrong . . . Lord, it seems like the floodgates of trouble have opened up on my life! Right now there's relationship turmoil, financial issues, and physical problems, just to name a few. I'm afraid to answer my phone or look around the next corner for fear of more bad news. Why is this happening? And what I want to know even more is when will it let up? I feel like I cannot handle anything else. Please have mercy on me! I am discouraged and frustrated. Please intervene. I need your help and your assurance that it's going to be okay.

These things I have spoken to you, that in Me you may have peace. In the world you will have tribulation; but be of good cheer, I have overcome the world.

—John 16:33

$\mathcal{F}$ather, a spiritual leader, one who professes to represent you, has left the high road of truth and love to follow a self-serving path. I feel so grieved and hope he will turn back, but right now what he is doing is hurting a lot of people. People who are new to the faith are disillusioned. People like me who supported and prayed for him are disheartened. And people from the outside looking in are shaking their heads at the hypocrisy of another of your so-called followers. Where can I find a place of worship where leaders are faithful to you—to your Word and your ways? Help me be that person first, no matter where I worship, but also please raise up faithful leaders who will take seriously their role of caring for your people.

*If we keep our focus on God, we'll keep
our feet when those around us go sideways.*

*I seldom think about my limitations, and they
never make me sad. Perhaps there is just
a touch of yearning at times; but it is vague,
like a breeze among flowers.*
—Helen Keller

At certain times I'm painfully aware of my
weaknesses, Lord God, especially when the people
around me possess strength in the areas where
I feel deficient. Insecurity and melancholy start
eroding my peace and joy when others around
soar as I falter along. Even as I say these words,
though, you remind me that comparison is
unwise. You make us each unique with our own
sets of strengths and weaknesses so that we can
appreciate and value one another and help each
other. You're a wise and benevolent Creator, and
I'll thank you for these weaknesses of mine, even

as I thank you for the ways in which I'm strong.
Let this disappointment be turned to praise even
now, because you made me just right.

You hold my eyelids open;
I am so troubled that I cannot speak.

—Psalm 77:4

$\mathcal{I}$ didn't realize, Lord Jesus, that the most difficult thing about relocating would be the lack of feeling connected. I'm adjusting just fine to all these unfamiliar places and ways, but I'm not sure how to adjust to the empty spaces in my week where friends used to be. At my age, most people have their circle of friends and aren't really interested in newcomers. And now in this loneliness, clouds of depression are gathering around my heart and mind. I realize that this is a time when I need to lean into you, to draw closer and come to know friendship with you in a new way. Help me shift my thinking toward discovery of dimensions of your love for me, rather than languishing in the loss of comfortable relationships. Thank you for being my best of all my friends.

If we are willing to receive them, the messages of love God sends us are more comforting, uplifting, inspiring, moving, delightful, and assuring than the words of a thousand silver-tongued poets, preachers, or paramours.

$\mathcal{I}$just wanted to tell you, Father, that even though this darkness presses in all around my soul, I sense your presence here with me. You keep me from despair, and you uphold me with your caring. Nothing in the world means more to me than the reality of you, the reality of your constant love. I don't know how long this sadness will linger. I don't know how far I have to walk before I see light again. But I do know that every second, every step, is seen and known and shared by you. And that is enough to see me through.

The presence of faith gives no guarantee of the absence of spiritual depression; however, the dark night of the soul always gives way to the brightness of the noonday light of the presence of God.
—R. C. Sproul, "The Dark Night of the Soul,"
Tabletalk Magazine

You will keep him in perfect peace,
Whose mind is stayed on You,
Because he trusts in You.

—Isaiah 26:3

$\mathcal{I}$ told a friend today that I cannot remember the last time I really laughed. I said this because while we were visiting, something did make me laugh so hard I cried. You saw us, Father God, as we laughed and cried together. And then I wept because my emotions have been so bottled up, and that incident was like opening a shaken can of soda. Thank you for that unexpected moment of relief. Thank you that my friend listened without judgment or trying to fix things with advice. That listening ear, the hug, and the promise to pray were just what I needed in the way of comfort and support. Thank you for the ways you encourage me through others. They truly are your hands and feet sometimes.

Embrace opportunities to be with empathetic people. You'll likely walk away from your time with them feeling warmly embraced in return.

Right now I feel like a dud, Lord. Of what use am I to anyone? I want to feel useful, not useless. I want to be a burden carrier, not the burden itself. Why are you allowing me to be sidelined like this? I can't bear it! If I can't be in the game, I don't want to be part of the team! Just take me home now! . . . Oh, Lord Jesus, I'm sorry. I'm throwing a tantrum, aren't I? If I truly trust you, then I have to trust that this is part of your plan for me. There is a reason for this—something I am to learn through it, and maybe something for others to learn as well. "Useful" doesn't need to look like my usual routine. As I yield to you, I will be useful in ways that matter most.

*What an encouragement to realize that God
has reserved you and me for a special task in
His great work. In His hands we're
not only useful, but priceless.*
—Joni Eareckson Tada

Who comforts us in all our troubles,
so that we can comfort those in any
trouble with the comfort we ourselves
receive from God. For just as we share
abundantly in the sufferings of Christ, so
also our comfort abounds through
Christ. If we are distressed, it is for
your comfort and salvation; if we are
comforted, it is for your comfort, which
produces in you patient endurance of the
same sufferings we suffer.

—2 Corinthians 1:4–6, NIV

$\mathcal{M}$y soul is destitute, Father. I'm crushed in spirit. I am sad beyond description. I can barely lift this prayer to you. I've nothing to bring you, not praise nor petition . . . just me standing here, needing you. Perhaps your Spirit will intercede for me, since I don't know what to say. There is that place in Psalm 23 that says, "He restores my soul." I suppose that is the hope I'm clinging to. I guess that is why I'm here. I believe you see me. I believe you hear me. I believe you love me. Here I am.

*H*e shall regard the prayer of the destitute,
And shall not despise their prayer.
—Psalm 102:17

Spending time in your Word, Lord God, as well as out in your creation, begins to push back the darkness that's been shrouding my soul. The light you bring is gentle, like the dawn gathering strength on the eastern horizon. Thank you for being so kind to me. Thank you for not giving up on me. I could not have made it through this time without you. I won't forget how you held me, walked with me, and carried me when I needed it. You showed me how to care for a hurting soul, and now I know how to love others who are hurting. Thank you. Bless you, Father. Amen.

When a journey through a dark valley in life comes to an end, we can look to our experiences there as a guide for knowing how to help others through the same dark time.

*H*e also brought me up out of a horrible pit,
Out of the miry clay,
And set my feet upon a rock,
And established my steps.

—Psalm 40:2

CHAPTER 2

Losing a Loved One

I do not want you to be ignorant,
brethren, concerning those who have
fallen asleep, lest you sorrow as others
who have no hope. For if we believe
that Jesus died and rose again,
even so God will bring with
Him those who sleep in Jesus.

—1 Thessalonians 4:13–14

$\mathcal{D}$ear heavenly Father, I feel so lonely now that my loved one has passed away. The days seem so empty, and the nights seem so quiet. Please, Father, remind me that I'm not alone. You are with me, and one day—because of your sacrifice— I will see my loved one again. Deepen my faith in my Lord and Savior, Jesus Christ. Lift up my spirit so that I can be a rock of strength to those around me. And guide me through these days of sorrow to a better place than I am in today. I pray in Jesus' precious name. Amen.

God assures us that death is powerless over us. When we die, we merely step over to a new life that is eternal and full of joy.

My flesh and my heart fail;
But God *is* the strength of my heart and
my portion forever.

—Psalm 73:26

$\mathcal{I}$ can't seem to stop crying, O God. The hurt is so deep. What am I going to do without my husband? He was my life. He took care of me, and he brought me so much happiness. He was my companion for so many years. Yes, we had our issues, but with your help we were constantly working on them. And through the years we became closer until we truly became one. I can't help but think about how he made me laugh and especially how he made me smile. I was so proud of him. More than ever, Lord, I need your love to get through this dark time in my life. Please hold my hand and comfort my heart.

$\mathcal{Y}$ea, though I walk through the
valley of the shadow of death,
I will fear no evil: for You are with me;
Your rod and Your staff,
they comfort me.

—Psalm 23:4

Lord, I believe a rest remains,
To all Thy people known;
A rest where pure enjoyment reigns
And Thou art loved alone;
A rest where all our soul's desire
Is fixed on things above;
Where fear and sin and grief expire,
Cast out by perfect love.

—Charles Wesley

The Lord *is* near to those who
have a broken heart,
And saves such as have a contrite spirit.

—Psalm 34:18

$\mathcal{S}$he was so dear to me, Lord Jesus. You gave her to me, and I cherished her as my loving wife for so many years. I am the man I am today because of her. I should have gone before her. Yes, I know that's very selfish of me. But I know she's with you, enjoying being with you, and preparing a place for me. She was so much better than me. Her faith in you was so much deeper. No man could ask for a better wife. I am a man of few words, but with those words I want to thank you for giving her to me. I long to be with her again.

The marriage between a man and a woman is one of the greatest blessings God has given to us.

Lord God, our mother was truly the bulwark of our family. She not only took care of our needs, but she also provided us with the spiritual wisdom that has guided us in our life journey with you. Whenever we strayed, she gently but firmly brought us back to you. Whenever we needed comfort, she was always there to wipe away our tears. And whenever we were at a crossroad in our lives, she shared the insights she had learned from you. Sadness fills our hearts because she is no longer with us, but we know that she is with you, and that, dear God, gives us abiding comfort.

My mother was the most beautiful woman I ever saw. All I am I owe to my mother. I attribute all my success in life to the moral, intellectual and physical education I received from her.

—George Washington

$\mathcal{D}$ad was awesome, Lord, because he wanted to be the husband, father, and friend you wanted him to be. Sure, he had his failings, but we always knew we could depend on him whenever we needed his help. We also knew that he loved you—and us. He may not have left his mark on the world like many great men, but he left a mark on us that we will always be grateful for. Dad lived a life full of tough challenges and rough hardships, and we're glad he is now resting with you. Nevertheless, Lord, we really miss him and will always honor him in our prayers.

Our heavenly Father is the perfect father.
Thank you, God, for guiding our earthly fathers.

A child should not have to go before her parents, heavenly Father. This girl was the light of so many lives. She had so much to live for. Her future was so bright! Why, Father, did she have to leave us behind? We just can't understand. We can't comprehend the wisdom of your plan. We cry out to you in our anguish. Please, Father, comfort us. We know this emptiness and grief will never fully go away, but help us live with the expectation that one day we will be with her again. Help us place our total trust in you. We pray in the name of our Lord Jesus. Amen.

O death, where is thy sting?
O grave, where is thy victory?
The sting of death is sin;
and the strength of sin is the law.
But thanks be to God,
which giveth us the victory
through our Lord Jesus Christ.
—1 Corinthians 15:55–57, KJV

What a joy, dear Lord, he was to us! So full of energy and life! We can't believe this little boy is gone. It's like a horrible dream, hoping that we will wake up and he'll be back with us, hugging us and telling us how much he loves us. But it's not a dream. He's really gone. How are we going to cope with this painful reality? We have each other, and we have you. But is that enough? We can never touch him again or hear his voice. We can never put our arms around him or see him smile. At times, it does not seem that it's enough, but please, almighty Lord, give us the faith that you are taking care of him and us.

God knows the pain of losing a beloved son;
he understands and grieves with us.

*H*e heals the brokenhearted
And binds up their wounds.

—Psalm 147:3

You know more than anyone, God, how deep our friendship was. We shared a treasure chest of wonderful memories. Though we lived many miles apart, we still talked on the phone often. And although her illness was unexpected, I'm thankful that we could chat a few days ago. Still, God, I miss her and will always miss her. She was such a joy in my life. I can't help but cry even now as I pray, thinking of her. Please keep reminding me of your promise that you prepare a place for each of your children. I would like a place very near hers.

*The footsteps of a godly man
can never be erased.*

This man was one of my best friends, heavenly Lord. He taught me so much about life and how to be true to one's own principles even when worldly forces try to turn us against your holy precepts. Although I fought with him now and then, he was unquestionably my hero. I looked up to him and always will. Most of all, I admire the way he served you by helping those in need, and he always did it cheerfully and sometimes even sacrificially. Yes, he was a very good man. Thank you, Lord, for the gift of him in my life. Now help me to follow the example he lived so I can have peace about his death, even though I'll always miss him.

Farewell, sweet maiden; at thy tomb
My silent footstep oft shall stray;
More dear to me its hallow'd gloom,
Than life's broad glare, and fortune's day.
—James Grahame, "On the Death of a Sister"

I know, Lord Jesus, that I shouldn't be forlorn over an animal. But he spent more time with me than any person. He showed me more love as well. Sure I took care of him—providing him with the right food and a warm place to sleep. And he returned that care with sincere affection, never complaining, always seeking my approval. You are, after all, the Lord of all creatures. So may I ask—will he be in heaven with me? I truly hope so. He was more than a pet; he was my loving, sweet companion; he enriched my life in every way. Thank you, Jesus, for giving him to me these past few years.

*Our furry friends are the Creator's gift
to humankind. Let us not worship them
but treat them as precious gifts from
our beloved Father in heaven.*

$\mathcal{B}$lessed are those who mourn,
For they shall be comforted.
—Matthew 5:4

$\mathcal{A}$t Grandma's service, there were so many people who cried so many tears. So many people, Lord, loved her deeply. I can't count the number of people who told stories about how she touched their lives. Throughout her life, she placed her trust in your holy Word. She loved to read the Bible; she loved to memorize the verses that were especially meaningful to her; and she loved to recite them to us. And now she can listen to you face to face. It is so comforting to believe that! Nevertheless, it's really difficult to see her empty chair. Dear Lord, we need your encouragement to help us through this time of grief and sorrow. We pray in Jesus' holy name. Amen.

The legacy of our ancestors is passed down from generation to generation. How glorious is that legacy when those ancestors were women and men of God!

Grandpa was so much fun to be around, heavenly Father. I remember when he carried us on his shoulders and chased us around the house. He was there for us, even from a distance. He told us how smart we are and how pretty or handsome we are. He gave us many gifts, but the most precious gift was his tender affection. Spending time with Grandpa is one of our fondest childhood memories. We'll miss Grandpa, Lord. Please take care of him, and please always remind us how he enriched our lives. Help us pay homage to a truly great man by having the faith he had in you.

*B*lessed *is* the man
Who walks not in the counsel
of the ungodly,
Nor stands in the path of sinners,
Nor sits in the seat of the scornful;
But his delight *is* in the law of the Lord,
And in His law he meditates
day and night.

—Psalm 1:1–2

*Jesus loved children and welcomed
any who wanted to sit with him.*

God, it's too much to bear the loss of a child. We feel so much pain and so much anger. She was such a happy child—full of innocence and goodness. She had so many dreams for herself, and she had so much love for people and animals. It's not right that she was taken from us! And yet, our faith tells us that she was a precious gift you gave us—her time here was far shorter than we wanted—but she was still a wonderful gift. Help us cherish her in our hearts. We so need your help at this very sad hour.

Jesus wept.
—John 11:35

To live in the hearts we leave behind is not to die.

—Thomas Campbell

*H*e's gone, dear Jesus. The disease finally took him. We cry and cry and cry, knowing that we can no longer hold him. But the tears can't wash away the pain in our hearts. He was so dear to each one of us. We loved the way he laughed when he was having fun and the way he showed his pride when he did something right. He was even endearing when he made a mess. Oh, how can we survive another day without him! Only in you, precious Jesus, can we find the strength to go on. So please take care of him until the time when we can all be together again.

*H*e will wipe every tear from their eyes.
There will be no more death or mourning
or crying or pain, for the old order
of things has passed away.

—Revelation 21:4, NIV

She will never be forgotten. She was joyfully gracious to each one of us, Lord. I don't think we ever thanked her enough for all the wonderful things she did for us. Please, Lord, let her know that we are deeply grateful and will always remember her generosity and warm hospitality. Even more, we're so grateful for her years of prayers for us. She truly was a spiritual advocate for each one of us. And I believe she is still lifting us up in heaven. Thank you for this marvelous woman, and please help us through these sad days without her. We pray in Jesus' holy name. Amen.

*All spiritual gifts are vital to the church, and
the Lord has endowed each member with the
ability to pray. And yet, those who have the
gift to pray on behalf of others because of their
intimacy with you are to be especially honored.*

Today, Lord, we pray for those who were
killed serving others. Police officers put their
lives on the line every day so our society can be
safe. Many of these brave men and women leave
behind families. That's hard to understand. I
pray for these families today, Lord. As much as
we're hurting, their pain is a hundredfold. Please
comfort them, and show us how we can help.
And help us believe that you are all powerful and
in control and that your justice will ultimately
prevail. Meanwhile, help us through this tragedy.

*My heroes are those who risk their lives
every day to protect our world and make
it a better place—police, firefighters
and members of our armed forces.*
—Sidney Sheldon

*A*lmighty Lord, we come before you, asking for solace in this time of deep grief, for our beloved friend has crossed from this world to the next. He was such a caring friend to all of us. I speak for our entire family when I say there will always be an empty place at our holiday and family gatherings, particularly at Christmas when he demonstrated the spirit of Christ like no other person we know. The wind feels especially cold and the clouds appear especially dark right now, but he taught us to trust you to wipe away our tears during times like this, and so we shall, heavenly Lord.

We honor those who have gone on before us
to your waiting arms in your heavenly kingdom
because they have left us a life to emulate
in our earthly journey with you.

*R*ecord my misery;
list my tears on your scroll—
are they not in your record?
—Psalm 56:8, NIV

*W*e had been friends for decades, Lord Jesus. Although our backgrounds were different, no two people could be more alike in religious views and views about the world. Oh, Lord! When I heard she was sick, I couldn't believe it. And when she breathed her last breath, I couldn't help but break down. What am I going to do without her? She is so precious to me! Lord, Lord, I need you. I want to be with her. Oh, Lord Jesus, fill me with your love and assurance that you will heal my heart and someday reunite us. She's in heaven now, and for that I am truly grateful.

How can there be a heaven without our loved ones, but more importantly without the one who has truly taught us to love— our Lord and Savior Jesus Christ!

God, my friend was so merciful, but he wasn't always so compassionate. But when he gave his life to you, you transformed his character into the man you wanted him to be. And during that time, we became brothers in Christ; in fact, we became great friends. At his work, he was one of only a few Christians, and although he exuded warmth and kindness, he was often ridiculed. Even his family did not take his faith seriously. Nevertheless, he didn't react with anger or bitterness; he displayed Christian love. I admired him for that, but even more I will miss his special friendship.

The righteous perishes
And no man takes it to heart;
Merciful men are taken away,
While no one considers
That the righteous is taken
away from evil.
He shall enter into peace;
They shall rest in their beds,
Each one walking in his uprightness.
—Isaiah 57:1–2

Serving one's country is a great honor,
but an even greater honor is serving the one true God.

The solider just wanted to serve our country. He lost his life on the battlefield performing the highest duty a citizen can perform. Dear God, we are all proud of our friend. But even greater than his sacrificial patriotism was his dedication to you. He gave his life to you, and since then he has been serving you and others by showing the people around him how to be like Jesus. Now that he has found rest in you, help us honor him not only with sadness but also with the zeal to be more like your beloved Son. Amen.

So many people loved her, Lord Jesus. She meant so much to so many people. And it's because your love always overflowed from her to everyone around her. If there was an angel among us, she was that angel. And now, Lord, you've called your angel home. Our hearts ache, knowing that she won't be greeting us at church and sending out her cheery emails. She had a way of brightening the day no matter how gloomy it seemed. Today, even the daytime seems like nighttime. But the radiance that glowed from her soul is not gone because you are still with us. Remind us, dear Jesus, of that. She surely would want us to go on with that belief in our hearts.

The pain passes, but the beauty remains.
—Pierre Auguste Renoir

Lord God, how can we cope with this loss? He was more than a friend; he was a spiritual mentor. So much about what we know of you and Jesus we learned from the wisdom he taught us. Both his insights and his counseling have been our sails and our rudder while your breeze has pushed us forward through the ocean of life. Now, Lord, how are we to go on without this gentle and kind man, so strong in his faith in you and so dedicated to serving us? We know he is with you, so please turn to him and tell him that we miss him, that we love him, and that we will always cherish him in our hearts. In Jesus' precious name, we pray. Amen.

The hands that molded us will never let us fall and break; we are too precious to the Master Potter.

Dear heavenly Father, you must have a special place for firefighters in heaven, and that's where our friend is right now, for she died putting out a destructive fire. We joke that the devil wouldn't let our friend in his neighborhood; she would be putting out all the fires there. But we know she is with you. Now she doesn't have to extinguish fires anymore but can enjoy her well-deserved retirement. She was a great friend, Lord, and we'll miss her loud laughter and silly jokes. Most of all, we'll miss singing hymns and songs with her. Please lift up our hurting spirits, we pray in your holy name. Amen.

*They sacrifice their today
for our better tomorrow.*

CHAPTER 3

Surviving a Catastrophe

O you afflicted one,
Tossed with tempest, *and* not comforted,
Behold, I will lay your stones
with colorful gems,
And lay your foundations with sapphires.

—Isaiah 54:11

O Lord God, this horrible disaster has really been a blow to my family and me. It was so unexpected. One day, everything is fine; the next day, everything is gone. Our extended family, friends, and church all want to help us, and we are truly grateful for their generous compassion, but still we feel utterly defeated. A lifetime of hard work is wiped out, and now we have to start over. Please help us, Lord, to be thankful that we have our lives and each other, and most importantly, that we have you to take care of us. Help us, we pray in Jesus' precious name. Amen.

Though the night is dark and gloomy,
the sun will rise and bring a brighter day.

$\mathcal{G}$od *is* our refuge and strength,
A very present help in trouble.
Therefore we will not fear,
Even though the earth be removed,
And though the mountains be carried
into the midst of the sea;
Though its waters roar *and* be troubled,
Though the mountains shake with its swelling.
—Psalm 46:1–3

What has happened to me, Lord Jesus? I can't comprehend the calamity that has overwhelmed me. I still can't believe it happened to *me*. So many times on TV I've seen catastrophes happen to other people, and I felt deeply sorry for them, but I never thought it could happen to me. I can't stop repeating with disbelief, "It has happened to me! It has happened to me!" Lord, I know my zeal to serve you has not been as it should be, but I promise to be faithful to the leading of your Spirit. Just help me now, Lord! Please give me hope and strength to go on.

Sometimes your medicine bottle has on it, "shake well before using." That is what God has to do with some of His people. He has to shake them well before they are ever usable.

—Vance Havner

As I look at the devastation around us, mighty
God, I can't help think that the forces of
nature have turned our neighborhood into a
battleground. Our homes are destroyed, and our
belongings are swept away. I wonder if we can
rebuild our community. But we must! We can't
allow ourselves to feel as though we're helpless

victims, because if we do, then we've lost more than our material possessions. And yet, we can't do it on our own. We need your strength and guidance to get us back on our feet. And so, Lord, we pray that you will take control of our hearts and minds as we work to rebuild. And most of all, help us help one another.

Alone, I can do little; together, with God's help, we can accomplish much.

I will lift up my eyes to the hills—
From whence comes my help?
My help comes from the Lord,
Who made heaven and earth.
—Psalm 121:1–2

*T*his, heavenly Father, has humbled me as nothing else has in my entire life. I always believed that I could take care of myself. In fact, I always thought I could do better than anyone else in my family or my friends. But now I need their help to get me through the mess I'm in. It's hard to ask for help. I was always the one people came to for assistance, and I would gladly lend a helping hand. Was it pride or sincere caring on my part? Now that I'm the one who needs help, I know that if ever I'm the giver again, it will be out of true compassion. So, in a way, thank you, Lord, for teaching me this lesson. Most of all, it's you that I need, and so, I humbly come to you to take care of me.

*A true servant of God is one who gives
humbly, selflessly, and cheerfully.*

The outdoor beauty you created near us, God, has been destroyed. It may take a generation or longer for some of it to come back to life, but in the meantime, we will no longer be able to enjoy it. We try not to be angry at what occurred, and only you can assuage our bitterness, but it's really hard to accept this calamity. Only you, God, can bring good out of tragedy. Please fill us with your peace and assurance that your hand is already at work replenishing the barren landscape. We thank you that you are our Creator, a Creator who bestows life in rich abundance. Amen.

They confronted me in the
day of my calamity,
But the Lord was my support.
—2 Samuel 22:19

𝒪 God, the desolation is too much for us! We can't believe you allowed this to happen. We've been so devoted to you. We've always done everything you've asked us to do. You've been the center of our lives and the God we've proclaimed to everyone we know. When others have gone their own way or turned against you, we've kept the faith. And still, the catastrophe has hit us. Why, God? Why us? O God, even if we can't understand why, please lift up our faith so we can trust you. Please embrace us with your love. We pray in the precious name of Jesus. Amen.

*It is not for us to understand the ways of God
but to trust in his abiding love for us.*

One catastrophe after another! Lord, it seems to never end. How can we cope with so many disasters? There's only so much people can take, and then they lose all hope. We're getting close to that point, but are there still more to come? We look at Job and see a man who suffered terrible calamities. He lost his possessions, his family, and his health, and we wonder whether we can be as faithful as he was. With just our own strength, we can't do it. We need your help to stay positive and hopeful. Please, help us anchor our faith in Jesus and cast all our fears and anxieties on him, our rock and our Savior.

Though He slay me,
yet will I trust Him . . . .
He also *shall* be my salvation.
—Job 13:15–16

Thank you, Lord Jesus, for saving us. We could have perished in the disaster, and so we're grateful for our lives. We're also thankful for our family and friends who have helped us through this horrible ordeal. Still, it all seems like a terrifying nightmare, and if we could only wake up, everything would be back to what it was. But it isn't what it was! Lord, now more than ever we need you. Please gather us in your arms and continue to shelter us from harm. Without you, we are hopelessly lost; with you, we need not fear, for we have your abiding love. Thank you again, Lord Jesus.

Darkness has fallen over us, but we have the light of God's love within us.

$\mathscr{I}$'ve never seen a catastrophe impact so many people, merciful God, and being in the middle of it has left me speechless. I can't find the words to describe the widespread suffering around us. I can't believe the government or even the church can rescue all of us—the devastation is unbelievably massive. We need you to protect us from further harm and the designs of evil people. Only you, God, can truly rescue us. The image I hold before me is that of a phoenix rising out of the ashes. Please give us the faith to believe that you will do this for us. We pray in the holy name of your Son. Amen.

I believe in Christianity as I believe that the sun has risen: not only because I see it, but because by it I see everything else.

—C. S. Lewis

My heart is steadfast, O God,
my heart is steadfast;
I will sing and give praise.

—Psalm 57:7

Oh God, the devastation has ravaged our land. Oh God, the desolation has rocked our world. The raindrops that wet our faces, are they your tears in response to our ordeal? Or are you far away, unaware of and indifferent to our plight? You are the Creator of the universe and all that is, and we are merely like the grains of sand on a boundless shore. Why would you care for us, especially since we are constantly in rebellion against you? When I think of your Son coming to earth from his princely realm to suffer and die for us, oh God, I know that you do care for us, and that your wondrous love is with us now during our time of great need. Hallelujah!

The Lord God is like a mighty ocean whose waves roar with resounding thunder. God's promises are even more loud and powerful. Surely he will save us from every calamity!

*B*e anxious for nothing, but in everything by prayer and supplication, with thanksgiving, let your requests be made known to God.

—Philippians 4:6

*H*oly God in heaven, nature has unleashed her fury against us, and now our home has been leveled to the ground. As we walk among the rubble, we come across a torn photo here and a broken toy there and little else. For many, many years, Lord, we worked hard to pay for this home. What a terrible loss! What a horrible blow! Oh God, help us recover from this disaster. We have nowhere else to turn. We have no one else who can rescue us. We humbly bend our knees in the rubble of our home and plead for your hand to lead us away from here to a better tomorrow. Thank you for your consoling Spirit. Amen.

*Our heavenly Father watches over us
in good times and bad.
We need him in both times.*

[Jesus said] "Therefore do not worry, saying, 'What shall we eat?' or 'What shall we drink?' or 'What shall we wear?' For after all these things the Gentiles seek. For your heavenly Father knows that you need all these things. But seek first the kingdom of God and His righteousness, and all these things shall be added to you."

—Matthew 6:31–33

$\mathcal{T}$he catastrophe, God, is more than I can bear. I can't understand why this happened to me. What did I do wrong to deserve this? Why am I being punished? Or are you teaching me something about myself and you? Am I being changed in some way to be more like Christ by this hardship? Or are you guiding me in another direction from the road I've been traveling? I have so many questions; they boggle my mind. Meanwhile, my heart is in chaos. I'm sorry for not having enough faith to rest in you, Lord. Please increase my faith. I pray in Jesus' precious name. Amen.

Faith does not eliminate questions.
But faith knows where to take them.
—Elisabeth Elliot

It is so hard, Lord God, to come to you right now. I know I'm feeling post-traumatic stress. It is extremely difficult to cope with the horrendous incident that recently occurred in my life. I want to scream from the pain in my soul. Oh God,

how can I get myself to turn to you? What hope
do you have to offer me? What promises can you
make to me? Part of me yearns to place my life in
your hands. But another part of me resists. Help
me turn to you for help! Help me find refuge in
you. Help me believe in your love for me.

*Prayer should be our first response to a
catastrophe; for those who believe
in the goodness of God, it should be the
natural reflex of our souls.*

*N*ow may the God of hope fill you
with all joy and peace in believing,
that you may abound in hope by the
power of the Holy Spirit.

—Romans 15:13

This disaster has taken my house. But, Lord, it hasn't taken my home, for you are my home. I praise you for being my protective abode. No matter what happens to my material possessions, nothing can take away my most important belonging. Nothing can take you away from me. And yet, it's still hard to believe this all the time. There are moments in which I get down and my heart sinks very low. I know these feelings are natural, and I don't want to be superficially happy. I just ask that your peace abide in me even when I'm low. You are a great God, and I will praise you forever.

 For I am persuaded that neither death
nor life, nor angels nor principalities
nor powers, nor things present nor
things to come, nor height nor depth,
nor any other created thing, shall be
able to separate us from the love of God
which is in Christ Jesus our Lord.

—Romans 8:38–39

The widespread wreckage around me, Lord, chills my bones. The silent aftermath is deafening to my ears. People stroll aimlessly about me, and stray dogs hunt for scraps of food. How can I help them when I have nothing myself? What can I do to alleviate the intense suffering before my eyes? I want to do some good, but I don't know how I can help. Lord, show me how I can be merciful, for I know if I help others I won't sink into despair. I suppose that sounds self serving, and I admit I'm not a remarkable person of faith. But your goodness motivates me to look beyond my situation and act in the service of others. So show me the way, Lord, and please minister to those in need through me.

When we receive God's mercy, we can't help but spread his compassion to others.

Mighty Lord in heaven, we need a stronger and deeper faith in you to get us through this awful calamity. It does not seem as though any power can raise us up from this disaster. Government and relief agencies can provide shelter and food, but they can't renew our spirit when we've lost everything. Only you, Lord, can give us the strength and determination to rebuild our lives. Nevertheless, it's not easy to trust in your promise to take care of us in all situations and under all circumstances. And so, we pray for a dynamic, transforming faith that will be a radiant light in our increasingly dark world.

Faith sees the invisible, believes the unbelievable, and receives the impossible.
—Corrie ten Boom

*A*nd my God shall supply
all your need according to His riches
in glory by Christ Jesus.
—Philippians 4:19

$\mathscr{A}$ dark shadow has fallen upon us, Lord God,
a shadow of catastrophic proportions. Where
is your light to guide us through this crippling
disaster? Our hearts and minds are so unsettled

that it's hard to see. We need you to grasp our hands and lead the way through the debris. Lord, our faith is weak, but you are our rock. Show us that life can be good again beyond our broken dreams and current troubles. The prosperity we seek is not in material possessions but in a closer walk with Jesus. He is our treasure, and that treasure we can never lose. Thank you, dear God.

A catastrophe will always challenge
our faith and define our character.
It will transform us for better or worse.
It will either draw us closer to God,
or we will allow it to diminish our faith.

The magnitude of this calamity, dear Jesus, is more than I can cope with. Today is one of the worst days of my life—maybe even *the* worst. I have endured setbacks before, but none compare with this catastrophe. I thought that nothing could shake my faith in you, but now I'm really being tested. Satan has a hold on me, and he is filling me with anger and bitterness. Please, Lord, break the hold he has on me. Free me of the destructive thoughts that he is casting into my mind. They are more damaging to me than even the calamity itself. Oh Lord, claim me as one of your own. I want—I need your love to shield me from the poisonous arrows of the devil. Keep me safe in your heavenly kingdom. I pray in your cherished name. Amen.

Evil is always lurking in the shadows,
but we stand in the light of the Son,
who drives away all darkness.

Continue earnestly in prayer, being
vigilant in it with thanksgiving.
—Colossians 4:2

We are in the midst of a cataclysmic disaster, almighty God. We have no place to run to except to you. Fear grips us. We cower and tremble in the face of nature's wrath. Our lives are at the precipice, and the ground beneath us is unstable. This calamity is challenging our faith. Oh God, help us keep our eyes on you despite the nearness of the threats. We're terribly afraid, but we will trust in your goodness. Harbor us from harm, instill courage in us, and clothe us with the honor that no matter what happens to us, we have placed our trust in you. We pray in the righteous name of Christ Jesus. Amen.

Calamity is the test of integrity.
—Samuel Richardson

Holy Father, it's really difficult to comprehend the reason for this disaster. Why did it have to happen? Why did so many people have to die? Why was the destruction so massive? I don't understand, Lord. Perhaps I never will. Despite my perplexity, however, help me rely on your wisdom—that all things work for good to those who love you, even when those "things" seem contrary to your goodness and your love for us. You have given me a brain to reason, but sometimes I am left only to trust in your providence. And this is one of those times. And so, I acknowledge your greatness and submit myself to your will for my life. Show me how to serve those in need and not question your great wisdom. Amen.

Yet, in the maddening maze of things,
And tossed by storm and flood,
To one fixed trust my spirit clings:
I know that God is good!
—John Greenleaf Whittier, "The Eternal Goodness"

I'm experiencing the dark night of the soul,
God, because of the calamity that has struck us.
Gloom is heavy upon me. Though my family
exhibits deep faith in you, I am unable to. I
want to, but this disaster has been too much
for me—not because of what it has done to me,
but because of how my family suffers from it.
It doesn't seem just and right that they have to
endure so much travail and hardship. And so,
God, my soul is in wretched anguish, and I am
stuck in an emotional quagmire. Please lift me
from this turmoil. Help me see that I am not
distant from you, but rather that this ordeal is a

time of transition in which you are taking us to a better place in our lives. Help me, God, to cling tightly to you.

*Our journey with God must pass through
spiritual crises in order to reach
the destination he has planned for us.*

The Lord *is* my light and my salvation;
Whom shall I fear?
The Lord *is* the strength of my life;
Of whom shall I be afraid?

—Psalm 27:1

Dear precious Jesus, I am in utter ruin. This
situation has devastated me in so many ways. I
feel crushed and alone. The inner joy that I felt
yesterday is torn to shreds today. Inner peace
is a stranger to me. I retreat deeper into myself

118

and find that the shadow of my soul is becoming increasingly darker. Dear Jesus, I need you more than ever. I am reaching out to you. Take my hand and rescue me. Oh Jesus, thank you for embracing me with your loving arms. Thank you for showering me with tender kisses. Thank you for wiping away my tears with your caring fingers. I praise you for taking on my burdens and for being my God and Savior. Thank you, Lord Jesus.

The Lord is my shelter from the storms of the world. I will abide with him for all eternity.

For I, the Lord your God,
will hold your right hand,
Saying to you, "Fear not,
I will help you."

—Isaiah 41:13

CHAPTER 4

Dealing with Economic Hardship

But You, O God the Lord,
Deal with me for Your name's sake;
Because Your mercy *is* good, deliver me.
For I *am* poor and needy,
And my heart is wounded within me.
—Psalm 109:21–22

Father, I am looking to you for what I need. I know that there is no ultimate security in pensions or property, lotteries or government programs, inheritances or investments. While you may use some of these at times in my life, they are faulty foundations on which to build my world. Only you hold the future in your hands; only you can provide for what the future holds. And your plan may look nothing like what I have envisioned or what the world considers sound. Help me place my trust squarely in you and leave it there as you lead me safely through these financial challenges. Whether help comes through the miraculous or the mundane, I know it is you who is providing for me. Thank you, Father.

𝒟o not put your trust in princes,
Nor in a son of man,
in whom there is no help . . . .
Happy is he who has the
God of Jacob for his help,
Whose hope is in the Lord his God.
—Psalm 146:3, 5

𝒥n this time of economic struggle, Lord, heal my perspective. Teach me to value only those things that are truly valuable and to be mindful of and thankful for your provisions each day. Thank you for my heartbeat, for daily meals, friendship, faith, a warm place to sleep, clothes to wear, and the assurance of your love. Money is a terrible god; it's fickle and it always requires more and more of me. I know that in a sense, it "makes the world go 'round," but I don't want it at the center of my world. I want you, the God of peace and perfect provision, to be the one around whom my world revolves.

The fellow that has no money is poor.
The fellow that has nothing but
money is poorer still.
—Billy Sunday

*H*elp me find things to be thankful for today, Father. I want to focus on what I do have, rather than on what I don't. Even if what is on hand is less than I'd like, help me praise you for every bit of your provision in my life. When I wake up in the morning, help me thank you, first thing, for as many things as I can think of. And before I put my head on my pillow at night, help me speak out my gratitude for every good gift from your hand. Wake me up to the blessings you've placed all around me, and through thanksgiving and praise, fill my heart and mind with faith that you will carry me through the days ahead.

A thankful heart . . . helps fortify the believer's trust in the Lord and reliance of His provision, even in the toughest times. No matter how choppy the seas become, a believer's heart is buoyed by constant praise and gratefulness to the Lord.

—John MacArthur,
Grace to You newsletter, March 2009

$\mathscr{B}$lessed is the one who perseveres
under trial because, having stood the test,
that person will receive the crown of life
that the Lord has promised
to those who love him.

—James 1:12, NIV

$\mathscr{P}$lease help me keep my integrity, Lord God,
in this financially tough time. Help me not to let
fear entice me to compromise what I know to be
right and good and true. There are people who
will do "whatever it takes" to get what they want
in life. I don't want to become like that. I want to
look in the mirror and not feel ashamed. As I put

my trust in you, even as others seem to get ahead by dubious means, help me rest in the knowledge that your plan for my life will prevail. You have good plans for me, and no one can thwart them by any means. Thank you for the strength of heart, soul, and mind that you gave me so I can live in a way that honors you.

Good character is a priceless possession.
Never give it a price tag.

𝒪h, Father! You see me on the days when I'm discouraged about my financial landscape. And in my foul mood, when I see good things happening for other people, I'm tempted to start decorating my soul for a big pity party. Instead of letting their blessings remind me that your timing is perfect and that you have good things in store for me, I start mentally whining: *Why them and not me?*

Forgive me, Father! I want to have a heart that can rejoice with others as though their successes were my own and to cry with them as though their sorrows were mine as well. Keep me free from self-pity and full of hope and trust in you.

Let your conduct *be* without covetousness;
be content with such things as you have.
For He Himself has said,
"I will never leave you nor forsake you."
—Hebrews 13:5

Father, I just realized that I'm so focused on the current struggle that I have not acknowledged your track record of provision and blessings before this turn of events. I know that when I remember history, it can often help in navigating the present as well as help in moving toward the future with a faith-filled heart and mind. Help me not avert my eyes from those better economic times, but to rejoice that they have been part of my experience, even helping to enrich this time of struggle as I learn to be content in your goodness, no matter what station in life I find myself. Thank you, Father.

God wants to see prayers that are filled with genuine praise and thanksgiving for what He has done in the past. He wants our hearts to be filled with awe and gratitude for His blessings. He wants us to set up memorials in our hearts testifying to the provisions He has given us.

—Michael Youssef

I have to tend to my financial realities, Lord. I know that faith does not mean neglecting them, but it's hard to look and not get nervous. Please help me to not be afraid. I need your wisdom and insight to think creatively, your direction to explore options and opportunities, and your encouragement to be proactive in finding solutions. I pray that you would help me keep my eyes and ears open to possibilities and to be bold in making inquiries. With your Spirit guiding my steps, I will not allow discouragement to keep me from doing the part you call me to on this journey of faith.

Keeping in step with God's Spirit requires that we not lag behind in fear nor run ahead in presumption, but that we walk steadily in faith, our eyes fixed on Christ.

I know what it is to be in need,
and I know what it is to have plenty.
I have learned the secret of being content
in any and every situation, whether well
fed or hungry, whether living in plenty
or in want. I can do all this through
him who gives me strength.
—Philippians 4:12–13, NIV

$\mathcal{I}$t's hard for me to ask for help, Father. I didn't realize until now that humility and humiliation are two very different things. Your example shows me that humility is gracious about needing help. But I feel humiliated at the prospect of seeking help because my pride gets in the way; it goes kicking and screaming against such an affront to my self-sufficiency. You're showing me, though, that I need to get over my pride and move toward humility, move toward leaning into others during this time when it has become necessary for me to do so. Forgive me for thinking of need as despicable rather than embracing it as a part of what it means to be human.

The give-and-take of helping and being helped is part of the interdependence God has built into our lives so that we can need and be needed without shame.

*A*nd I will do whatever you ask in my name, so that the Father may be glorified in the Son. You may ask me for anything in my name, and I will do it.

—John 14:13–14, NIV

I want to confess my attitudes of self-sufficiency to you, Father. As I seek you for help during this time of need, I realize how much I have neglected my relationship with you—how much I pushed you to the side, thinking there were more important things to pursue. I don't think you are trying to punish me for that; I just believe that in your mercy you intervened to stop me from getting too far away and getting lost in the shuffle of life. And you know, as bad as this financial situation has been, I am feeling more "on track" now that I've slowed down and have begun spending meaningful time with you, praying and reading your Word. It's good to be back.

Maybe you have suffered a financial loss and you find it very difficult to understand. Is God speaking to you in an effort to bring you back to Himself? . . . Face these matters squarely and be honest with God as He deals with you.

—Theodore Epp

When I read your Word, I see over and over again how you cared for your people—how you intervened in hopeless situations, providing protection and provision. Thank you for that written record of your goodness. Thank you that your character does not change no matter how much time passes; not even for all eternity will your faithfulness change! So I do not need to lose sleep. Even if the worst-case scenario unfolds, you are with me, and you have a plan. Help me let go of my notions about what the plan should look like and just peacefully trust you today.

You shall eat in plenty and be satisfied,
And praise the name of the
Lord your God,
Who has dealt wondrously with you;
And My people shall never be
put to shame.

—Joel 2:26

$\mathcal{I}$'m amazed, dear Lord, at how these financial limitations bring out the creative side of my thinking. I'm finding ways to make seemingly impossible situations workable. I'm becoming a bit of a creative solutions expert. (You know I'm smiling as I say that.) I want to thank you for the wisdom and the insight you are giving me and also for the creative abilities you have hardwired into my makeup as an individual. Your Word says that we are wonderfully made. And we are. I just wanted to marvel today at your creative power, as I delight in the creativity you've placed in me as your created work. I lift up my thanks and praise to you right now.

*Sometimes it takes a trial
to reveal a hidden blessing.*

For our light and momentary troubles
are achieving for us an eternal glory that
far outweighs them all. So we fix our
eyes not on what is seen, but on what is
unseen, since what is seen is temporary,
but what is unseen is eternal.

—2 Corinthians 4:17–18, NIV

$\mathcal{I}$t's a daily decision I have to make, Lord God, how I will respond to my financial circumstances. As you know, my first and most natural inclinations—to worry, to be irritable, to feel sorry for myself, to panic—are self-defeating, not to mention a lapse in trusting you. Thank you for your Holy Spirit who keeps watch over my thoughts and who speaks peace, truth, and comfort to my heart each day. Help me listen attentively as he reminds me of your Word. And help me respond with a childlike faith when he assures me of your loving care over my life.

God knows what each one of us is dealing with. He knows our pressures. He knows our conflicts. And He has made a provision for each and every one of them. That provision is Himself in the person of the Holy Spirit, indwelling us and empowering us to respond rightly.

—Kay Arthur

𝒟ear Lord, thank you for the empathy that is growing in my soul. This financial pain has awakened my heart to those who are doing their best to make ends meet and yet are struggling to get by. I "get" their plight now. As I look back on more prosperous times in my life, I can see where I might have helped some folks out a little by leaving a bag of groceries on their doorstep or dropping off an encouraging note with a sum of money. Let this lesson remain with me so that if I am able in the future, I will be more ready to open my heart and my hand to fellow travelers along the way.

*Where sympathy looks in
on a difficult situation and pities,
empathy looks in and understands.*

$\mathcal{D}$o nothing out of selfish ambition or vain conceit. Rather, in humility value others above yourselves, not looking to your own interests but each of you to the interests of the others.

—Philippians 2:3–4, NIV

*Y*ou assure me in so many ways, Father. I can't see around the next corner, but you are providing for me moment by moment. Thank you for this "daily bread" I've been receiving from your hand to meet each need. Thank you, too, for the huge billboard of creation that continually displays the message of your faithful provision. You've arranged it all so beautifully, and it speaks to me continually. The seasons arrive on cue with their respective provisions for all the flora and fauna, great and small. Your wisdom and attentiveness to every detail is profound, mind-boggling. Yet it is all elementary for you. And so is this situation I find myself in. Help me remember that today.

The eyes of all look expectantly to You,
And You give them their food in due season.
You open Your hand And satisfy the
desire of every living thing.
The Lord *is* righteous in all His ways,
Gracious in all His works.

—Psalm 145:15–17

Whether my financial situation takes a turn for the better or the worse, Father, I want to retell the stories of your daily faithfulness to me. I want to encourage others by describing what you've done. I want to tell it because it shines a light on your faithfulness—it gives you glory, and you deserve that. It's my way of praising you, even as I reassure others. Please help me remember—to chronicle and never forget—each little miracle along the way, each orchestration of events and circumstances that were just what I needed at a critical point. Help me speak up when I know the moment is right, and help me write down the highlights so they are never forgotten.

Honoring God by telling of his goodness
is a way we can bless him for all
the ways he blesses us.

For life is more than food, and the
body more than clothes. Consider
the ravens: They do not sow or reap,
they have no storeroom or barn; yet
God feeds them. And how much more
valuable you are than birds!
—Luke 12:23–24, NIV

There is the temptation, Lord, to feel powerless
when financial resources are not at my disposal.
But you are teaching me that the sense of power
I've sometimes had with money in my pocket has
been a superficial kind of power, a conditional,
changeable thing. I'm learning that true power
comes from you and is not tangible or subject to
the winds of change. Power to be at peace, power
to delight in life itself, power to find satisfaction
in truth and love and beauty—these are the powers
of contentment that can be mine at all times.
And it's the kind of power that no amount of
money can secure. Today, as you lead, I'll walk in
contentment. It's all the power I could want or
need in this life. Thank you, Lord Jesus!

*True contentment . . . is the power of getting
out of any situation all that there is in it.*
—G. K. Chesterton

𝒯ime is a priceless gift from your hand, Creator
God. Thank you for granting me the privilege of
a lifespan on this earth. Although I don't know
how long it will last, every heartbeat is a gift. And
now that my financial situation has changed, I'm
seeing that while I may not have extra cash to
buy things for people, I can give them a precious
parcel of time. I can listen to, laugh with, walk
beside, encourage, and nurture with the time you

145

have given me here. I can create spaces in the day for memories, reprieves, and prayer—whatever the situation may require, whatever might be meaningful to another. Here I am, Lord God. I'm putting at your disposal the gift of time you've given me.

Favorite memories in life most often include gifts of time others have given us.

*E*very good and perfect gift is from
above, coming down from the Father
of the heavenly lights, who does not
change like shifting shadows.

—James 1:17, NIV

*O*h, Lord, let my character be free from the love
of money; instead, let my heart be full of ever-
deepening love for you and others. During this
time of financial leanness, search my attitudes
toward money and material things. Please ferret
out what does not please you, the things I'm blind
to that poison my soul and my relationships. Your
Word says that a person cannot serve God and
money—that he or she will be devoted to one or
the other, but not to both. Those are sobering
thoughts, Lord Jesus. I don't want there to be
any rivals to your lordship in my life. Search
my heart and purify it so that I may serve you
wholeheartedly.

*It is the heart that makes a man rich.
He is rich or poor according to what he is,
not according to what he has.*
—Henry Ward Beecher

When I'm tempted to start feeling sorry for myself, Lord, help me find ways to serve others who are also struggling. You've shown me that it's not only a good way to find mutual support and encouragement, but it also takes the focus off of me and puts it on the blessing of community. In serving others, your Spirit opens my eyes to the truth that I am not alone in my struggle. Many others are struggling, and we can lean into one another as we make our way along. My financial hardship is just one of life's many burdens made lighter when I carry it in the context of fellowship in your name. Thank you, Lord.

*Immersing yourself in good community
when you're feeling down can be like
taking medicine when you're sick.
The medicine may be distasteful at first,
but the healing benefits will become
evident in just a little while.*

$\mathcal{A}$nd do not forget to do good and
to share with others, for with such
sacrifices God is pleased.
—Hebrews 13:16, NIV

$\mathcal{P}$riorities . . . Father, my priorities can get all
turned around with a single bit of troubling
news: an unexpected expense, a bill that is more
than I'd anticipated, a request for immediate
payment. When something like this comes up,
suddenly I'm focusing on it as if it were the most
pressing thing in the universe. Oh, dear Father,
help me step back. Help me see such things as
they truly are. They are not too big for you. You
are not wringing your hands, wondering how
you will possibly help me. The first thing I need
to remember and do is come to you, to present

my concerns and leave them with you. Then I can focus on what really does make the world go 'round: your truth and love flowing into my life and out toward those around me.

Whatever tests in life you're facing, whether it's a challenge of relationships, finances, or your career, the loving Spirit that created you is always available to guide you into a better life.

$\mathcal{I}$'m reminded, Lord Jesus, that when you walked this earth, you were a man of humble means. You were born to humble parents, your first bed was a feeding trough for animals, and during your years of ministry, you said of yourself that you didn't even have a home of your own where you could lay your head to rest. Your focus was on eternal things, not on things of the earth. Your hardships were not complaints for you but a chosen way that kept you unfettered from distractions. I am still learning to see my economic hardships as blessings in disguise that are leading me toward a better, more eternally focused way of life. Thank you, though, for your example that clearly shows me that true spiritual riches are available to me when I walk before you in a spirit of humble trust.

*E*ach of you should use whatever gift
you have received to serve others, as
faithful stewards of God's grace in its
various forms. If anyone speaks, they
should do so as one who speaks the very
words of God. If anyone serves,
they should do so with the strength
God provides, so that in all things God
may be praised through Jesus Christ.
To him be the glory and the power
for ever and ever. Amen.
—1 Peter 4:10–11, NIV

Jesus said, "Blessed are the poor in spirit"—
contrary to what we would expect,
brokenness is the pathway to blessing!
There are no alternative routes;
there are no shortcuts.
The very thing we dread and are tempted
to resist is actually the means to
God's greatest blessings in our lives.
—Nancy Leigh DeMoss,
Brokenness, The Heart God Revives

$\mathcal{G}$od of my life, I think of the righteous and wealthy Job in your Word, who, when everything was taken from him—his wealth, his children, his health—said, "The Lord gives, and the Lord takes away. Blessed be the name of the Lord." That is an amazing response to being utterly devastated. Job trusted you and worshiped you, even when his heart was heavy. He declared that he would trust you even if you struck him dead. Job truly was patient in his faith. His example speaks to my situation today. I want to have that kind of faith in this economic crunch; I want a faith that is willing to wait for you. You give, you take away, Lord God, and you provide what I need to keep going. Blessed be your name!

*Patience in our trials is the fruit of the
indwelling presence of God's Spirit.*

Be joyful in hope, patient in
affliction, faithful in prayer.
—Romans 12:12, NIV

Jesus, the lyrics in the hymn "Joyful, Joyful
We Adore Thee" call on you to "Melt the clouds
of sin and sadness," to "drive the dark of doubt
away," and they entreat you as the "Giver of
immortal gladness" to "fill us with the light of
day." O Jesus, this is my prayer! I want to be one
who can worship you with a heart full of joy on

the inside, no matter what transpires in the world around me—not because I don't feel or care about the losses and financial difficulties in my life, but because I know that at the end of the day you are still God, and I belong to you, and you are all I really need.

Joy has nothing to do with material things,
or with a man's outward circumstance . . .
a man living in the lap of luxury can
be wretched, and a man in the depths of
poverty can overflow with joy.

—William Barclay

$\mathcal{C}$onsider it pure joy, my brothers and sisters, whenever you face trials of many kinds, because you know that the testing of your faith produces perseverance. Let perseverance finish its work so that you may be mature and complete, not lacking anything.

—James 1:2–4, NIV

Chapter 5

Resisting Temptation

*N*o temptation has overtaken you
except such as is common to man;
but God *is* faithful, who will not allow
you to be tempted beyond what you
are able, but with the temptation will
also make the way of escape, that
you may be able to bear *it*.

—1 Corinthians 10:13

For me, Lord God, the temptations of the mind are stronger than the temptations of the heart. When thoughts of sinning linger in my mind, I can't help but imagine how pleasurable it would be to succumb to a particular temptation. As I dwell upon it, I start to fantasize, creating a scenario of how that sin would take place moment by moment. And with each moment, my resistance weakens until I'm nearly lost. Cast these corrupting thoughts from my mind, Lord. Focus my attention on you. Help me to pray, for when my attention is on you, only righteous thoughts occupy my mind, and sin has no power over me.

It is not enough to flee from temptation;
we must run to the Lord, or else
temptation will surely overtake us.

*T*herefore submit to God. Resist the
devil and he will flee from you.

—James 4:7

*H*eavenly Father, I want to be a faithful and
obedient child, but there are times when I'm
tempted to go my own way. I want to satisfy myself
rather than serve you. I want to be free of your
will to do what I please. My wants are terribly
selfish, I know, Father. I have such a long way to
go before I can be like the other men and women

of faith I know and I've read about. You have so much patience to deal with me. I'm sorry, Father, for causing you so much trouble. Please forgive me, and help me resist these ~~~~~~~~~~ and to act independently on ~~~~~~ to please you.

I do not want merely to possess a faith,
I want a faith that possesses me.
—Charles Kingsley

*Hold onto the Lord as if you are grasping onto
a rope as you hang over a towering cliff.*

*H*ow can I resist a temptation that I have
succumbed to time after time? My Creator, you
have made me in your image, and yet I behave
more like a beast who is out of control. Still,
it's only human to be sinful—or so my worldly
friends tell me. Something that feels so good
can't be so wrong! Our desires are who we are.
Right? Wrong! You have told me that I must
live a morally righteous life—even though it goes
against my tendency to please myself. I must stop
myself from surrendering to these temptations,
and instead I must surrender to your will. I must
place my life in your hands. But I can't do this on
my own. I need your strength to resist and your
holiness to be pure. Please clothe me in your
righteousness.

$\mathscr{W}$atch and pray, lest you enter into temptation. The spirit indeed *is* willing, but the flesh *is* weak.

—Mark 14:38

$\mathscr{W}$herever I go, Lord, some kind of temptation always confronts me. It could be as common as driving down the road and being tempted to be angry at another driver. Or it could be as uncommon as seeing someone in distress and being tempted to ignore that person. No single temptation is difficult to resist. It's the constant onslaught of temptations that wears me down. And when I'm fatigued and haggard, I just feel that I can't help myself. Oh Lord, please continue to wash me of my sins. Cleanse my heart and my mind. And give me the power to repel evil and conquer the temptations that daily besiege me. I pray in the precious name of Jesus. Amen.

In this world, we clash against evil daily.
Faithful believers in Christ can never let their
guards down. And so, we should be as
wise as Jesus commanded us to be.

For in that He Himself has suffered,
being tempted, He is able to aid
those who are tempted.
—Hebrews 2:18

The devil is like a hungry lion that seeks to devour my soul, God. And if I continue to give in to temptation, he will succeed. Deliver me from the evil one so I can live faithfully and obediently. The time has come for me to step up and be true to your Word. I want to serve you and not be tripped up by the temptations the devil throws at me. I know that each time I fall, you will pick me up, but I want to make you proud to be my Father. Holy God, I pray that your scriptures will shield me from evil and inspire me to do all things according to your will.

*The Bible recognizes no faith that does not
lead to obedience, nor does it recognize any
obedience that does not spring from faith.
The two are at opposite sides of the same coin.*
—A. W. Tozer

*T*ake captive every thought to
make it obedient to Christ.
—2 Corinthians 10:5, NIV

*O*h God, I'm being tempted beyond my strength
to resist. Please deliver me from this situation.
I know that I willingly walked into this situation.
I lied to myself and you, believing I would
not be tempted to sin, but for me, in fact, the
temptation is irresistible. I suppose, God, I'm
tempting you to get me out of this mess. Jesus
said not to put you to the test, but I have. God,
please forgive me. I have been thoughtless and
careless with my faith in you. Please turn me
away from sin, and help me walk on the path of
righteousness. I pray in Jesus' name. Amen.

*Prayer and other believers can be the
best defense against temptations.*

Sin beckons me, Lord Jesus. It is a clear and present danger to my soul. How can I silence its enticing voice? I not only hear it, but I also listen to it. It speaks to me in words that are familiar to me. It has an intimate knowledge of my weakness. Oh Lord, help me not yield to it. Remind me that it has no dominion over me. You have given up your life for me so that I can be faithful to God. Moreover, your Spirit dwells in me to empower me to live under grace. Your words are what I want to hear. Your words are what I will listen to. Thank you, Jesus, for delivering me from sin.

For sin shall not have dominion
over you, for you are not under
law but under grace.
—Romans 6:14

Prayer is my best refuge from the temptations of the world, holy God. When sin comes knocking at my door, that's when I turn to you, for then my resolve to be faithful is strengthened, and

I am safe from spiritual harm. Thank you, God, that you are not a distant god, but a God who is always near to listen to my pleas and my reflections. Thank you, God, that you are not an impersonal god, but a God who cares for me and loves me deeply. Thank you for adopting me and claiming me as your dear child. Loving God, may my prayers be constant and sincere and full of gratitude for all eternity. Amen.

Prayer is the mighty shield that wards off the poisonous darts of the evil one.

For all that *is* in the world—the lust
of the flesh, the lust of the eyes,
and the pride of life—is not of
the Father but is of the world.

—1 John 2:16

$\mathcal{L}$ord God, you know how difficult it is for me to bridle my tongue. It's so easy for my tongue to react to people or a situation in a way that's not pleasing to you. I often say things without thinking, and I hurt people. Sometimes I *want* to wound people for one reason or another. The temptation to speak unkindly is sometimes hard to resist. Help me, Lord. Give me the overwhelming desire to please you and not myself. I know that if my thoughts and emotions are anchored in you, the temptation to utter destructive words will vanish. I know that I should not blame my tongue for my transgressions, for my tongue can be used to praise you and uplift others. It's what's in my heart that comes out of my mouth. So transform my heart so that my words will be a reflection of Christ's goodness.

Remember that the tongue speaks
only what is in the heart.
—Theodore Epp

*Give all your thoughts to God, and he will lead
you on the path of righteousness.*

$\mathscr{L}$ord, the temptation to sin is so much easier in
the digital age. I can say things and do things in
secret. Only you know what I do when I behave
badly on my computer or some other electronic
device. Shame is a strong deterrent against sin.
But when nobody knows what I do, shame has
less power to curb my evil desires. And yet, what I
think is just as secretive as what I do electronically
in private. I now know why Jesus said what we
entertain in our head is the same as committing
the sin in our behavior. So, if I think on heavenly
things, I won't be tempted to sin in my mind or
while working at a keyboard. Please, Lord, help
me submit my mind to Christ.

If we confess our sins, He is faithful
and just to forgive us *our* sins and to
cleanse us from all unrighteousness.

—1 John 1:9

Dear Jesus, please take my hand and lead me
away from this temptation that has unexpectedly
emerged before me. It's these temptations that
pop up from nowhere that are most troubling to
me. My faith might seem strong, basking in your
light, and then suddenly a shadow will fall on me
and temptation will spiritually blind me. Dear
Jesus, help me! Keep my focus on your teachings.
Empower me with your Spirit. And strengthen
my resolve to remain obedient to your will. I
know that temptations are everywhere in this
world, and it would be impossible to live without
them before I enter your heavenly kingdom. And
so, Lord Jesus, I place my life in your hands to
keep me safe from sin and evil. Amen.

Let the gale of God's Spirit blow into your sails to take you in the right direction.

There would be no temptations, heavenly Father, if they had no appeal to me, which indicates to me that sin still has its hold on me. Oh Lord, the most lethal temptation is to believe the devil's lie—that I'm still in his clutches and am hopelessly lost. This is what temptation does to me; it robs me of my confidence in your promise that you have claimed me as one of your children. Remind me of this truth every moment of my life so that my walk with you will be filled with joy and peace rather than with doubt and guilt. Thank you, Father, for showering me with your abiding love. Amen.

God loves you just the way you are,
but He refuses to leave you that way.
He wants you to be just like Jesus.

—Max Lucado

*Y*ou therefore, beloved, since you
know *this* beforehand, beware lest you also
fall from your own steadfastness, being
led away with the error of the wicked.

—2 Peter 3:17

*M*y pride, God, is my greatest weakness. I can't help but think that I'm smarter than most people. So when I'm disrespected, I'm tempted to strike back in some way. Even with my family and friends, I do not tolerate even the most innocent slight. I don't know why I'm this way. I know that I shouldn't be. I know that this trait of mine is in stark contrast to the fruit of your Spirit. And I also know that it only causes me grief when I give in to the temptation to hate—even if only in my thoughts. God, forgive me for wanting to hurt people. Forgive me for being so proud and arrogant. Please help me to be kind and gentle. I would be so much happier if I were. I pray for this in Jesus' holy name. Amen.

Too much pride is harmful
to our spiritual health.

For if anyone thinks himself
to be something, when he is nothing,
he deceives himself.

—Galatians 6:3

The temptation to want others to serve me
rather than the desire to want to serve others,
Lord, has been my preoccupation during this
time of my life. I feel as though I deserve to be
served, having always put others first for much
of my life. How can this be wrong? And yet, I
know that it is if I'm truly to be your faithful
servant. Such a selfish desire as I feel right now
has no place in your kingdom, and I must display
humility in whatever I do or say. It's not that I
shouldn't ask for help when I need it. I know,
Lord, you want us to serve one another and that
you don't want me to display false humility. So
please shift my feelings of self-indebtedness to
what you want me to do for others.

For you, brethren, have been called
to liberty; only do not *use* liberty
as an opportunity for the flesh,
but through love serve one another.

—Galatians 5:13

Sometimes, God, I wonder why believers still must face powerful temptations. Hasn't the blood of Christ cleansed us of sin once and for all time? Doesn't the Holy Spirit dwell in us to guide our lives and inspire us to live righteously? Don't we want to obey and please you? So why don't you stand between us and evil at all times? Why do you allow us to fall? I suppose it's because you don't want to turn us into robots or puppets, and you want us to mature spiritually into adults who choose to serve you despite all the sins and temptations in the world. It's still very difficult for me to comprehend your ways, God, but I choose to follow you anyway because my only hope is in you.

The Lord God is the Creator and
absolute ruler of the universe.
To him be glory and praise forever.

*D*o not be overcome by evil,
but overcome evil with good.

—Romans 12:21

*N*o sin is so tempting that you can't shield me from it. And so, Lord, I'm asking you for your protection from this sin that's tempting me now. I just don't have the inner strength to resist it on my own—as you know. Please come and yank me from this situation. I know that your grip on me might be so tight that it hurts, but I call for you anyway, Lord, because falling into this sin would be far worse for me. Thank you for watching over me and for being my champion. My life would be such a mess without you. Thank you, Lord God.

*The distance between God and ourselves
is not measured by how many temptations
we encounter but by how often we turn
to God to resist those temptations.*

$\mathscr{A}$s much as I would like for you, God, to change my circumstances so I'm no longer being tempted to sin, I realize that what I really need is for you to get me through these circumstances. I suppose what is more important than any change in my situation is a change in me. Thank you for reminding me that your greater purpose is to transform my character into the character of Christ. Instead of dealing with the symptom of my problem, you seek to treat the source of my problem. I praise you, God, that your design for me is focused on my need and not on my want.

Often times God demonstrates His faithfulness in adversity by providing for us what we need to survive. He does not change our painful circumstances. He sustains us through them.
—Charles Stanley

If you abide in Me, and My words abide
in you, you will ask what you desire,
and it shall be done for you.

— John 15:7

*L*ord, I am really tempted to turn my back on
people, particularly the person who has been
nasty to me. It's so hard to forgive, but I know I
must if I'm not to fall prey to this temptation to
be cold to people. This temptation is like poison.
Once it gets into my system, it preoccupies and
pollutes both my thoughts and my emotions,
and then I let it affect my actions. Lord, I need
for you to be my physician. Please treat my
affliction by giving me a forgiving and kind spirit
so I myself can be a prescription of your love to
others, especially to the person I regard as my
enemy. I make this urgent request to you in the
name of my Savior, Christ Jesus. Amen.

God is more than our friend; he's our healer.

*W*ho Himself bore our sins in His own
body on the tree, that we, having died
to sins, might live for righteousness—
by whose stripes you were healed.

—1 Peter 2:24

$\mathcal{I}$ get really frustrated and impatient, God, when things don't go the way I think they ought to. It's so tempting for me to be like this because, as you know, this is how I naturally am. Without your hand on my life, I would be a mess. I know it. And that's why I come to you right now, for I'm starting to get frustrated and impatient with my current situation. Please remind me that I can rest in you and trust that you are in control of my life. Help me, God! I am weak and need your strength to get me through this. Rescue me from myself. I pray in your name. Amen.

*Our life voyage is an exciting adventure
kept on course with Jesus at the helm.*

$\mathcal{D}$ear heavenly Father, this temptation is
different from any that I've faced before. I
didn't think I could be tempted in this way, but
now I need you to deliver me from doing this
wicked deed. And yet, I want to do it. The urge
is nearly overpowering me. I thought that I had
taken precautions not to be where I am today,
but here I am, vulnerable to such an enticing
temptation. Father, please keep me on the path
of righteousness. I *do* want to please you rather
than myself, but I need your Holy Spirit to keep
me pure and faithful. Turn my eyes from this
temptation to your holiness, I pray.

Sometimes, Lord, I think that if I give into the temptation, it won't bother me anymore. But I know that a temptation is like an itch. Scratching it won't make it go away, and often it makes the itch even more intense. And that's how it is with temptations. And so, Lord, help me overcome this itch to do what I know is contrary to your will. Instead, create in me a greater desire to be obedient to your will and to live a holy life. Thank you, Lord, for already having conquered the source of all temptations. I claim that victory in Christ right now for myself.

Submitting to temptation enslaves us to sin.
Submitting to Christ, however, liberates us
from the bonds of evil.

For the Lord knows the way
of the righteous.

—Psalm 1:6

$\mathcal{L}$et no one say when he is tempted,
"I am tempted by God"; for God
cannot be tempted by evil, nor does
He Himself tempt anyone.

—James 1:13

*W*hy, heavenly Father, do I at times think that *you* are tempting me—that *you* are challenging my faith in such a severe way that you know that I'll stumble unless I rely on you completely? Is it because such challenges will strengthen my faith? I just can't believe that you use sin and temptations as tools to mold me. Instead, such thoughts are in fact devious arrows of the evil one to pierce my faith in your goodness and your love for me. Help me, Father, to believe firmly that you don't tempt me to sin but that such thinking is a temptation in itself to get me to doubt you. Thank you, Father, for being a righteous and gracious God.

The beautiful thing about this adventure
called faith is that we can count
on Him never to lead us astray.
—Chuck Swindoll

Now faith is the substance of
things hoped for, the evidence
of things not seen.

—Hebrews 11:1

My Lord God, help me resist temptation! Help
me stay on track! You, Lord, are my salvation and
my rock. Please anchor my faith in you alone.
Please take total control over my life. You are a
great God, and I praise you as my Master and the
Creator of all that's good and wonderful. Thank
you for adopting me as your cherished child. I
love you and thank you most of all for your Son,
Jesus Christ. For without him, I am nothing. But
with him, I am everything I could wish to be. Oh
Lord God, I pray all these things in the name of
my precious Savior, Christ Jesus. Amen.

Jesus knocks at our doors. Let us invite him in so that we might feast with him and experience eternal joy in his divine presence.

Ask, and it will be given to you;
seek, and you will find;
knock, and it will be opened to you.

—Matthew 7:7

CHAPTER 6

Facing Turmoil and Uncertainty

And the Lord, He *is* the One who goes
before you. He will be with you,
He will not leave you nor forsake you;
do not fear nor be dismayed.

—Deuteronomy 31:8

From where I am standing, Father God, I have serious concerns about the future of our society. I'm seeing that the standard of right and wrong that used to unify us is quickly giving way to an anything-goes approach. I believe this puts us on shaky ground. What will become of future generations without the clear boundaries of your Word and the clear direction of your truth? Help me, Lord! Encourage my heart with reminders that you are able to reach hearts that, though immersed in the cultural chaos of relativism, can by your Spirit find a firm foundation in your good and eternal ways.

Never be afraid to trust an unknown future to a known God.

—Corrie ten Boom

*A*nxiety in the heart of man
causes depression,
But a good word makes it glad.

—Proverbs 12:25

197

$\mathcal{P}$olitical news is among the most distressing, dear Lord. You know what I'm talking about: projections of economic collapse; rumors of corruption, greed, and deception; a political machine that no longer works effectively. What is going to become of the freedom—the wonderful rights and responsibilities—I've always enjoyed as a citizen? The winds of change are blowing in directions I fear. And, Lord, some days I feel like donning that sandwich board I see in comic strips: "The end is near." Ah, but you remind me in Psalm 2 and Psalm 33 that even when human powers rise up and presume to do evil, you will not allow them to prevail. You are the King of kings and Lord of lords. And as a citizen of your heaven, I will entrust my time on earth to you.

*L*et all the earth fear the Lord;
Let all the inhabitants of the world
stand in awe of Him.
For He spoke, and it was *done*;
He commanded, and it stood fast.

—Psalm 33:8–9

*M*y situation is uncertain, Father. The only
control I have in the matter right now is how I
choose to approach it. Will I stress and wring my
hands and have the background noise of anxiety
running through my head all day, even when I'm
doing other things? Or will I take a deep breath,
acknowledge the reality, and then choose to trust
you to show me the way through it? That is the
choice before me; that is the role I must play.
Help me not to run ahead with presumptions but
to wait and proceed as you clear a path for my
feet. If you have actions for me to take or words
for me to say, I trust you will make those clear to
me. I'm choosing right now to trust you.

*Every tomorrow has two handles. We can
take hold of it with the handle of anxiety
or the handle of faith.*

—Henry Ward Beecher

My life is in upheaval right now, Father. With
everything rolling through my mind, it's hard
to fall asleep at night; then it's hard to wake up
and face it all again. Where do I put my feet so I
stand firm? Where can my heart get assurance?
Where can my mind find peace? No place in my
outer world offers any semblance of security right
now. But in my inner world, in this place where
I come to meet you, I find you are still here:
steady, strong, faithful. You are my place to stand,
my place of peace. And I'm here right now to
find the rest my soul so desperately needs, to be
strengthened by you so I can face the day.

There is nothing more needful to our whole being than our daily solitude with God and his Word.

Therefore I tell you, whatever you ask for in prayer, believe that you have received it, and it will be yours.
—Mark 11:24, NIV

$\mathcal{D}$ear Lord, when I look at a "simple" blade of grass and consider how many such blades you cause to grow all over the earth, I realize the miracle is so common I can easily miss it. Yet can I make one blade of grass—just one—come into existence from nothing, as you did when you made the heavens and the earth? I cannot. Remind me again, Lord, that you effortlessly sustain the whole universe and everything in it.

You see it on the largest and smallest of scales, and you attend to every detail without straining your power one bit. Why do I worry, then, that you won't take care of what concerns me today? I will come to you, even now, and unburden my heart. Then I'll crawl like a young child into your everlasting arms and trust you to carry me. Thank you, Lord of my life!

> *And* which of you by worrying can add
> one cubit to his stature? If you then
> are not able to do the least, why are you
> anxious for the rest?
>   —Luke 12:25–26

To spend time praising you, Jesus, is like a strong antidote to whatever is burdening my heart. When I lift up my voice to praise you, in word or in song, the heaviness in my soul lifts too. I know your Word says that you give "the garment of praise for the spirit of heaviness" to those who belong to you. I guess that's a more poetic way of saying it, but however it's said, it's true! Your Word is true. Praise seems counterintuitive when things aren't going well, but when I trust your wisdom and just do it, it works every time.

We would worry less if we praised more.
Thanksgiving is the enemy
of discontent and dissatisfaction.

—Harry Ironside

Praise Him for His mighty acts;
Praise Him according to His
excellent greatness!

—Psalm 150:2

I worry about this loved one of mine, Father. He wanders far from you and is endangering his soul by rejecting your truth and your ways. I know we each have a choice to make as to how we will respond to your truth and love. I pray, though, that you will persistently make yourself known to him, as though you were sending personal notes signed with your own loving hand. Your Word says that your kindness is meant to lead us to repentance. I pray that my loved one will be able to perceive the many kind messages you send his way. Help me entrust to your kind heart this one who is dear to my heart as well. In Jesus' name I pray. Amen.

A popular lapel button worn in the 1970s
touted the letters PBPGINFWMY, shorthand
for "Please be patient; God is not finished with
me yet." It's still a good reminder that God is
always at work, not only in our lives but
also in the lives of those we love.

$\mathcal{D}$ear Lord, I'm not sure what my future will be employment wise. The economy is struggling, unemployment is high, and good jobs are hard to find. Will I be employed six months from now? I don't know. That's such a difficult uncertainty for me to live with. How do I map out a future from here? Do I buy things now in case they're not available in the future, or do I save as much as I can? Do I take calculated risks, or do I play it safe? I need your wisdom, Lord, to make decisions today, because you can see the future. I also need your peace and assurance today, because I cannot see the future. Guard my heart and mind in Christ Jesus. In his name I pray. Amen.

There are no guarantees for the future except the promises God has made. And they are the only guarantees we truly need.

Worry and anxiety are exhausting, Lord Jesus. All those "what ifs" steal the pleasure of the blessings I have today. Please forgive me for the times I've given in to fear, allowing it to steal my joy. Help me focus on the wonderful promises you've made in your Word. Teach me to reach for things of eternal worth, rather than for temporal things that come and go like the tide. Remind me that although life here on earth is full of the ebb and flow of change, I can put my trust in you—the one who is the same yesterday, today, forever.

*Anxiety does not empty tomorrow
of its sorrows, but only empties
today of its strength.*
—Charles Spurgeon

𝒩ow may the Lord of peace Himself
give you peace always in every way.
The Lord *be* with you all.

—2 Thessalonians 3:16

And those who know Your name
will put their trust in You;
For You, Lord, have not forsaken
those who seek You.

—Psalm 9:10

There's so much I need to get done today! The stress of my schedule has me all keyed up. I was tempted to push aside my appointment with you, Father. But then I felt like I couldn't afford to. You are the best part of my day, the most meaningful and needed. To miss fellowship with you is to miss my essential nourishment for life, to go forward without being focused, to enter the fray spiritually unprepared. I need you. I need to talk with you. I need to hear you. I need to know you are near. So here I am. Thank you for always being here for me. Heavenly Father, I love you so!

*J*esus answered and said to her,
"Martha, Martha, you are worried and
troubled about many things."
—Luke 10:41

*O*h, Lord! You know how difficult confrontation is for me! The terrible feeling in the pit of my stomach gets worse with every tick of the clock. Please help me! I want to be effective in this situation: kind yet firm, understanding yet unyielding when I need to stand my ground. Please give me your peace of heart and mind.

When the time comes, help me not unravel, not lose my resolve or my train of thought. Lord Jesus, I need your wisdom, insight, and boldness to speak truth in this situation. I pray you would go before me, prepare the way, and work within me as I speak. I pray my approach will honor you. I'll leave the outcome in your hands.

To truly love, we cannot be nice at the expense of being true. To be like Jesus, truth and love must never be separated from one another.

*L*earn to do good;
Seek justice,
Rebuke the oppressor;
Defend the fatherless,
Plead for the widow.

—Isaiah 1:17

I'm so anxious to know what lies ahead. The suspense is almost more than I can take, Lord. Instead of trusting that you're going to work things out, I'm worried it might not turn out as I'd hoped. But if I did know the future, I'd probably lie awake worrying about that, wouldn't I? Ah, Sovereign Lord! What is my relationship worth if I don't have faith in your goodness and power and love for me? I lay these worries at your feet—once again. Forgive me for picking them up over and over. You are worthy of my full confidence.

*God has wisely kept us in the dark concerning
future events and reserved for himself the
knowledge of them, that he may train us up in
a dependence upon himself and a continued
readiness for every event.*

—Matthew Henry

With the media coverage reaching all across
the globe, Lord God, I'm more aware than ever
of how an ordinary life can be altered in mere
moments. In the news I see accidents, natural
disasters, fires, thefts, fraud. And it seems as if
there are more and more angry, out-of-control
people harming others. How do I remain wisely
cautious without crossing the line into fear
or paranoia, Lord? I don't want to be always
looking over my shoulder, but I do want to be
responsible. Please grant me your insight and

wisdom—and even "gut" feelings if I need them— that will help direct me through danger. Cover my life with your protective care; I will trust you in all things.

In this fallen world, danger and harm are real, but so is God's protective power. Perhaps in eternity we will be permitted to see just how many times God rescued us from imminent danger without our even knowing it.

$\mathcal{A}$nd do not fear those who kill the body but cannot kill the soul. But rather fear Him who is able to destroy both soul and body in hell. Are not two sparrows sold for a copper coin? And not one of them falls to the ground apart from your Father's will. But the very hairs of your head are all numbered. Do not fear therefore; you are of more value than many sparrows.

—Matthew 10:28–31

$\mathscr{L}$iving God, as I focus on these Goliath-size threats of what is about to happen, my courage is faltering. Like that giant of long ago, my present circumstances seem to shout taunts at my faith and defy the promises I've been holding on to from your Word. Please, help me! Goliath was fearsome, but one lad with his focus on how great you are was able to rout him in your name. These hazards are not threatening to you. I need to keep my eyes fixed on you. Then my "Goliath" will seem small in comparison. Thank you, Lord God, that you are for me.

The objects of the present life fill the human eye with a false magnification because of their immediacy.
—William Wilberforce

$\mathcal{S}$omeone I love is going through a tumultuous time, Father. I don't know what to do, but I'm grateful I can pray to you, since you do know. You see how much I want to offer comfort and relief, how I'm wringing my hands, so to speak. Please show me how I can minister your love to her in tangible ways. Oh, Lord! I know we tend to blame and question you when things go badly (and sadly, we don't often thank you when things are going well). Please have mercy on my loved one's anger and her questions and fears. Help her know that you are near, that you love her, and that you are able to heal her if she will open her heart to the grace you hold out. Draw her, I pray, into your love as only you can do.

There is no greater intervention on behalf of another than to call on Almighty God to help them.

$\mathcal{F}$or I know the thoughts that
I think toward you, says the Lord,
thoughts of peace and not of evil,
to give you a future and a hope.

—Jeremiah 29:11

One day at a time, Lord, right? However much I might wish to rush into the future or retreat into the past, it is only this day, this moment that you call me to live in. I cannot undo what's been done, and I cannot control what is yet to come. And while those things are out of my hands, you have given me the power to do three vital things right now: to forgive and seek forgiveness for the past, to choose wisely right now, and to entrust the future to you. By your grace, Lord Jesus, I will do these things today, and I won't fret about the rest. Amen.

The future is something which everyone
reaches at the rate of 60 minutes an hour,
whatever he does, whoever he is.
—C. S. Lewis

The pressure is on, Lord, and this task before me seems like Mount Everest. I'm stressing out, and I'm near panic. If I panic, I'll become unproductive, paralyzed even. Please, dear Lord, come calm this anxiety about my fear of failure, of letting people and myself down, of being ashamed. Help me focus and move forward, taking one piece of the task at a time. Please help me work efficiently and effectively, doing my best and leaving the outcome in your hands. You're reminding me even now that if I trust in you and give a sincere effort, I have not failed, no matter how this turns out.

Success in God's eyes has everything to do with integrity, honesty, humility, love, faithfulness—all the characteristics that reflect his Son and bring honor to his name.

Commit your works to the Lord,
And your thoughts will be established.
—Proverbs 16:3

My need for security has stayed with me all my
life, Father. You saw my childhood; you saw the
times security was present and when it wasn't.
I used to think that when I grew up I'd have
life figured out or that at least I'd be the one
in control. And now that I'm grown, it seems I
understand all too well how much I don't have
figured out and how little I am able to control
in this world. Thank you for being my heavenly
Father, for showing me what the true nature of a
good father is like. You protect, you provide, you
nurture, you listen, you correct, you teach, you
assure, you encourage. And all of this you do in
perfect love, in tenderhearted affection. When I
come to you, you calm my fears and wipe away my
tears. You are my security, Father.

Where does your security lie?
Is God your refuge, your hiding place,
your stronghold, your shepherd,
your counselor, your friend, your redeemer,
your saviour, your guide?
If He is, you don't need to search any
further for security.
—Elisabeth Elliot

There are new things to learn on my horizon, Lord Jesus. As you know, learning curves are not my favorite thing. The older I get, the more tempting it is to stay in my comfort zone, but I'm grateful for this new challenge. I admit that I'm anxious about being able to catch on as quickly as I need to. But you've brought this opportunity my way, and I know that if you bring me to something, you'll also equip me to do it. Please help me leave my pride behind and humbly accept that I may make mistakes, I may need to ask questions that seem silly to others, and I may need to ask more than once or twice. I'll not worry about what other people think of me; I only have to remember that you love and accept me.

*Having the courage to try a new thing
is far more important than having
the ability to succeed at it.*

Wait on the Lord;
Be of good courage,
And He shall strengthen your heart;
Wait, I say, on the Lord!

—Psalm 27:14

Dear Lord, when problems come out of
nowhere and blindside me, my first response is
not always a faith-filled one. You know it usually
takes a little time for me to get my spiritual
equilibrium—to remember that you're still in

charge, that you saw it coming, and that I don't need to worry. I get there sooner than I used to, but I still have so much growing to do. Help me prepare my heart and mind for life's big "ambushes" by practicing with the small ones. When some minor frustration happens, help me call on you and walk through it with your guidance. As I practice on these little surprises, hurts, and difficulties, I'll be more prepared to respond to the big ones. Thank you for the ways you use my trials, even the small ones, to help me learn and grow in faith.

$\mathcal{D}$o not be afraid of sudden terror,
Nor of trouble from the
wicked when it comes;
For the Lord will be your confidence,
And will keep your foot
from being caught.

—Proverbs 3:25–26

$\mathcal{F}$ather, I keep fretting over what's in the past.
I wish with all my heart I could go back and do
things differently. A second chance isn't what I
wish for; I long to redo the first one, only with
the understanding I have now. The grief in my
heart can be unbearable sometimes. I know
you have forgiven me, but I am having trouble
turning my heart away from regret and toward
hope. Please, I need you to heal this brokenness
and help me receive your peace for the present.
Help me believe your promise that there is joy
just ahead.

Leave the broken, irreversible past in God's hands, and step out into the invincible future with Him.

—Oswald Chambers

℘ife seems always to be mailing out invitations to come to the place of worry. Yet in your Word, Lord, you tell me not to be anxious about anything but instead to pray about everything. That's why I know that, until the day I come to live with you in heaven, I will always be praying. Even now you see the things I'm tempted to worry about. By your grace, I'll turn my face away from fear and instead turn toward faith in you. Your comfort and peace are mine to enjoy as I rest in your strength today and always.

*Prayer is the only "worry stone" a
believer will ever need.*

𝒫eace I leave with you, My peace
I give to you; not as the world gives
do I give to you. Let not your heart be
troubled, neither let it be afraid.

—John 14:27

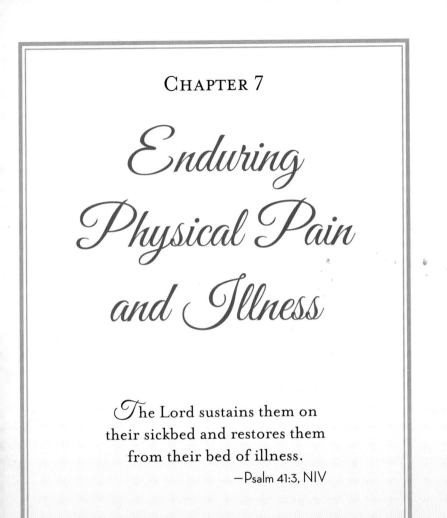

CHAPTER 7

Enduring Physical Pain and Illness

The Lord sustains them on
their sickbed and restores them
from their bed of illness.
—Psalm 41:3, NIV

Oh Lord, the pain is unrelenting today. Not even painkillers are helping. Please deliver me from my awful wretchedness! What do you want me to do in order for you to respond to my pleas? How do you want me to pray? Surely you can't bear to see me in so much agony? Oh Lord, display your love for me by ridding me of this piercing pain! My Lord, please forgive me for being presumptuous. The pain is so severe I can't think straight. I know that more than anything I need you beside me to sustain me. I know this pain is temporary and what awaits me is eternal joy in your heavenly kingdom.

At times physical pain can be absolutely horrible, but there is always an end to it. And for believers, the joy to come will make us forget our current earthly ordeals.

And not only that, but we also glory in tribulations, knowing that tribulation produces perseverance; and perseverance, character; and character, hope.

—Romans 5:3–4

Heavenly Father, I'm not good at enduring physical pain. I'm afraid that if I were tortured by terrorists, I would say anything they demanded of me. Sadly, I would probably even curse you. I'm sorry, Father, that I'm so weak. I wish I were a stronger Christian. In most every other way I think I am. It's just this one glaring flaw in my character. My uppermost request is that your Spirit empower me to keep the faith no matter how much pain I'm in. And let me not fear my pain. Please, Father, when I'm in pain, help me consider how it's nothing compared to how much Jesus suffered for me. Please keep my focus where it should be, on my Savior.

No person has suffered anywhere near what Jesus suffered, and he did it willingly for our sake. Let us never forget that.

This illness has been my companion for a long time, Lord Jesus. I've prayed countless times for it to leave me, but it remains nevertheless. I've been told just as many times that no answer to my pleas is still an answer from you and that you're not ignoring me. But, Lord, I still wonder why you won't heal me. I read about your compassion for the sick in the gospels, and they give me both hope and disappointment—hope because you can heal and disappointment because I haven't been healed. Please, Lord, increase my faith in you—not so much for you to heal me but to remind me that you are doing what is best for me. I pray that this illness will draw me even closer to you.

The greatest Christians in history seem to say
that their sufferings ended up bringing
them the closest to God—so this is the best
thing that could happen, not the worst.

—Peter Kreeft

*H*e gives power to the weak,
And to those who have no might
He increases strength.
Even the youths shall faint and be weary,
And the young men shall utterly fall,
But those who wait on the Lord
Shall renew their strength;
They shall mount up with
wings like eagles,
They shall run and not be weary,
They shall walk and not faint.

—Isaiah 40:29–31

*L*ord, how I hate being sick! It's hard to function when I'm this way. Not only do I feel lousy, but I also don't want to spread my illness to others. And so, I feel both unwell and isolated. I suppose being sick and alone is a perfect time for me to commune with you—to share what I'm thinking and feeling and to listen to what you want me to know and do with my life. Thank you, Lord, for grabbing my attention in this way. Otherwise, I might be too busy to hear what you have to say to me. Please keep me grounded in you. I pray in Jesus' precious name. Amen.

The words of the Lord are like soothing waters flowing over our souls.

Almighty God, my suffering has brought me to my knees. It has stricken me with a piercing and unrelenting pain. Even my bones creak from this physical torment. Help me, God, to endure this ordeal! Only you can bring relief. Only you can release me from this affliction. You are an awesome God who does mighty works. Please deliver me from my suffering. Please rescue me now! And yet, holy God, in your wisdom I will trust. In you, I will be content to bear my physical burdens while sharing them with Christ. For only in Jesus will I have inner peace for my soul.

It is not right to say that all suffering perfects.
It only perfects one type of person . . . the one
who accepts the call of God in Christ Jesus.
—Oswald Chambers

*I*s anyone among you sick? Let him call
for the elders of the church, and let them
pray over him, anointing him with oil
in the name of the Lord. And the
prayer of faith will save the sick, and the
Lord will raise him up. And if he has
committed sins, he will be forgiven.

—James 5:14–15

Such sickness as I feel right now, Lord God, is worse than I have felt in a long time. I almost want to die from the agony in my head and body. I have gone to the doctor and taken medication. Meanwhile, loved ones have attended to my needs, but I don't feel any better. I wonder if I'll ever get over this illness. It only seems to get worse. Please, God, listen to my prayers and take away this vile affliction. I want to be honest with you, and that's why I say these things. But I also want to be steadfast in my faith in Christ. So please, God, give me a humble and gentle spirit in order that I can be a reflection of your merciful love to others.

Even storm clouds cannot stop
the rising of the sun.

*B*ut He *was* wounded
for our transgressions,
He was bruised for our iniquities;
The chastisement for our peace
was upon Him,
And by His stripes we are healed.

—Isaiah 53:5

*D*ear Jesus, though I'm feeling pain, my prayer is for a joyful heart. I don't want people to see my physical hurt; instead, I want them to see your presence in my life. But I don't want to come off as being only superficially happy. I want to feel genuinely jubilant, so others can be blessed—not by me—but by you. I do not want to pretend that I'm not in pain either; I just want to show others that I am elated to be your friend and servant despite my infirmity. What better medicine than to have your abiding love nurse me back to health! I praise and thank you, Lord Jesus, for being my incomparable physician.

A cheerful heart is good medicine.
—Proverbs 17:22, NIV

I don't feel good, Lord. I am sick. My illness has gotten worse today, and it's hard for me to function and think clearly. Friends and family want to visit me, but I don't want visitors—not the way I feel right now. I certainly wouldn't be a good host. Oh Lord, why do I have to feel this way? I don't want to be a recluse, but I don't want to clean up and get dressed and entertain people either. I lack the energy. Please, Lord, keep me company. With you, I don't have to do all those things. You accept me even if I'm disheveled and grumpy. And you listen to all my complaints with patience. Please stay with me.

*Jesus has the patience and the desire
to be with us during our darkest hours.*

*H*eavenly Father, the pain from this recent injury is debilitating because it prevents me from doing my job. Should I go to the doctor? I hesitate because it's so costly to see a physician, and the medicine itself is an additional expense. More importantly, shouldn't I rely on you to heal me? What should I do? The pain is becoming increasingly unbearable! The more I meditate on this question, the more you remind me of Luke, the Gospel writer, who was a physician and attended to Paul while he was in prison. Dear Father, send me to a doctor like Luke, who was your servant and a servant to others. I pray in Jesus' name. Amen.

We praise God for Christians who are members of the medical community. They are his ambassadors who attend to the needs of every person.

The thief does not come except to steal, and to kill, and to destroy. I have come that they may have life, and that they may have *it* more abundantly.

—John 10:10

I wonder, Lord, how effective are my prayers? No matter what I say and how many times I say them, aren't you going to act according to your plans anyway? So what's the use asking you to heal me of this illness? In fact, the more I pray and the longer I remain sick, the more I feel discouraged and the more I lose hope that I will ever feel better. And yet, when I pray—if I'm really praying and not reciting a repeated request—I sense your presence. I still feel ill, but I also feel closer to you. And so, praying does have a purpose—a very important purpose: It leads me to you.

Health is a good thing; but sickness is far better, if it leads us to God.
—J. C. Ryle

There's no relief for my pain, God. Perhaps there never will be while I'm here on earth. And so, God, I ask that you give me the strength to bear it. I also pray that I won't be satisfied with my condition, but that I will always have hope for healing. I know that through your merciful grace, a miracle can happen and I can be pain free. I also know that in your wisdom I might not be released from this pain. God, help me keep my trust in your love for me. Increase my faith in Christ, and use my suffering for your glory. As I'm being pressed by this pain, I want to be an example of compassion to others. Thank you, God, for using me this way.

May we always be an aroma of Christ's gentleness and kindness so that others will be drawn to our Savior.

$\mathcal{B}$less the Lord, O my soul,
And forget not all His benefits:
Who forgives all your iniquities,
Who heals all your diseases,
Who redeems your life from destruction,
Who crowns you with lovingkindness
and tender mercies.

—Psalm 103:2-4

This physical affliction, Lord, is like a snake wrapped tightly around my soul, squeezing the life out of me. It stares at me with cold, deathlike eyes, and it hisses at me with its snarling tongue and sharp fangs. I feel helpless and frozen in its grasp. Not only is the hurt intense, but I'm also gripped with fear that my suffering will become even worse. Lord, please deliver me from this ghastly serpent! I'm in need of immediate rescue, and I cry out for the help only you can bring to me. Help me, Lord! I pray in the name of my precious Savior, Jesus Christ. Amen.

Many *are* the afflictions
of the righteous,
But the Lord delivers him
out of them all.
—Psalm 34:19

$\mathcal{M}$y Lord Jesus, I'm hurt. It happened so suddenly and without warning, and now my body is wracked with pain. Both my teeth and fists are clenched, and I shiver from its acuteness. Help me, Jesus, bear this! Shift my focus from me to you. Let it not overwhelm me with bitter rage. Instead, deepen my trust in you, and stir my affection for you. Lord Jesus, I praise you over and over again for being a God who cares for me—so much so that you were willing to suffer far greater pains than this for me. Thank you, Jesus, for understanding my pain. And thank you for holding my hand at this time.

*Jesus is our humble Master, who caringly washes our souls **and** our feet.*

*B*y faith in the name of Jesus, this man whom you see and know was made strong. It is Jesus' name and the faith that comes through him that has completely healed him, as you can all see.

—Acts 3:16, NIV

$\mathcal{P}$hysical suffering is the most challenging trial to my faith, holy God. When I was younger, it did not bother me much. I took it as just another hurdle to leap over in my daily activities, but now this hardship preoccupies me. I attend to it as the most dedicated nurse attends to his or her patient. It's as though it has fused into my being and is now part of my personality. God, I don't want to be like this. I don't want my physical condition to define my character. I want to be energetic and vibrant. And yet, God, if you want me to be physically weak so that you might be spiritually strong in me, than that's what I want as well. I just don't want that weakness to be the center of my life. I want you to be.

$\mathcal{H}$e said to me, "My grace is sufficient for you, for My strength is made perfect in weakness." Therefore most gladly I will rather boast in my infirmities, that the power of Christ may rest upon me.
—2 Corinthians 12:9

Sometimes, Lord God, I think that my infirmity is a curse upon me—that you've judged me and that you're punishing me for some sin I've committed. I know you're a loving God full of compassion and mercy, but I also know you're a righteous God intolerant of sin and wickedness. And I'm far from being pure of heart and mind. I know that at times I've displeased you, and I'm truly sorry for my wayward behavior. But above all, I believe in your grace and forgiveness, and I believe that through my infirmity you're not punishing or cursing me but teaching me how I can serve you more faithfully. Thank you, God, for blessing me in every way.

Our Lord is a gracious God, who takes delight in our faithfulness.

This was to fulfill what was spoken
through the prophet Isaiah:
"He took up our infirmities and
bore our diseases."
—Matthew 8:17, NIV

$\mathcal{I}$look upon my physical disability, Lord Jesus, as a gift—usually! I admit there are times when I'm frustrated and disheartened. Those are the times I compare my health to others and wonder why me? Instead of feeling that I'm a special witness for you, I feel like an unlucky victim of fate. Thank you, Lord Jesus, for understanding my sorrow and not being angry or disappointed with me. Thank you for your patience and gentleness and kindness toward me. I need you more than I can ever know. Dear Jesus, I love you with all my heart and soul.

Even though I have rough moments in my wheelchair, for the most part I consider my paralysis a gift. Just as Jesus exchanged the meaning of the Cross from a symbol of torture to one of hope and salvation, He gives me the grace to do the same with my chair.

—Joni Eareckson Tada

Today, God, I feel so sick! Not only does my body feel really wretched, but also I'm more concerned about my health than I usually. I suppose I'm afraid about what is happening to me. Am I getting worse? Or am I just having a really bad day? I wish sometimes this was merely a nightmare and I would wake up to find I'm not sick. But I know this is not a bad dream. My illness is real. And so, God, calm my fears, and if it be your will, please heal me. I so want a healthy body. Help me want a strong faith even more. I pray in Jesus' holy name. Amen.

Of course, spiritual health is far more important than physical health. Nevertheless, God grieves deeply when we are suffering.

𝓛et us then approach God's throne of grace with confidence, so that we may receive mercy and find grace to help us in our time of need.

—Hebrews 4:16, NIV

The pain, heavenly Father, is more than I can bear. I cry out in agony, but the pain does not lessen. Tears do not help, either. Oh Father, please give me relief! Hear my prayers! Listen to my pleas! I desperately need your help. I can't take it any longer. The pain is too great for me. And yet, even in my misery, heavenly Father, I will praise you. You are a great God, and I place all my trust in you. This pain will not deter me from praising you. It will not lessen my faith in you. I will not falter, for you are my fortress. You are my sanctuary. I feel your hand of mercy on me now, and my gratitude is beyond words.

*The heavenly host shout praises to our Lord
God. Join this angelic chorus and be lifted up
from the pangs of your suffering.*

Because of my illness, God, I know my family
sometimes feels put out when I ask for help. It's
as though they think I want to be sick so they have
to wait on me, and you know that's not true. I
hate being sick, and even more I hate needing
other people's help. I wish I could take care of
myself, but I can't. Do they think I like seeing
them rolling their eyes or hearing their sighs of
annoyance? God, please help me be forgiving and
gracious despite their exasperation. It's so hard
to be that way when I feel so poorly, but with your
help I can be like Christ, who was scorned even
when he was on the cross. I want to be more like
Christ, my Lord and Savior. Amen.

Is anyone among you suffering?
Let him pray. Is anyone cheerful?
Let him sing psalms.

—James 5:13

Lord, something is wrong with me physically. I can't believe it! I was hoping it was nothing, but now my doctor has confirmed it. And it's really serious—really, really serious. Lord, this news has floored me. I'm at my wit's end. Lord, please help me cope with this illness. I turn to you because you have always helped me through hardships, and though this situation is probably worse than any I dealt with before, my confidence in you is not shaken. I know you will take care of me, one way or another. Moreover, only you give me the hope I need to deal with my sickness. Thank you, Lord Jesus, for being with me now when I need you most.

Without hope, we cannot truly live.
Without God, we cannot truly hope.

*W*henever I'm in pain, Lord Jesus, I tend to rationalize it until I can endure it. But this time I can't. The pain is too severe. My mind has no power over it. Jesus, it's overwhelming! Please help me not give up. I can't go on without you. I truly know that now. The pain is great, but you are far greater. Thank you for lifting my spirit and for strengthening my faith in God. You are awesome! I don't necessarily pray for a miracle to relieve me of this pain but for a vision as to how I can be more like you and for a purpose as to how I can serve you better. I sing your praises, Jesus, because you are my Master and Deliverer.

Don't give up because the pain is intense right now. Get on with it, and before long you will find that you have a new vision and a new purpose.

—Oswald Chambers

The angel of the Lord encamps all
around those who fear Him,
And delivers them.

—Psalm 34:7

$\mathcal{P}$hysical suffering, almighty God, is something I'm not good at. I would rather die and be in heaven with you than endure intense pain, particularly what I feel at this moment. But, God, if I must continue to suffer, please carry this unwanted burden with me. In fact, I need you to carry most of my burden, for I'm too weak to bear it myself. You are a gracious and great God, and I thank you for your merciful love. I come to you now, confident that you will not abandon me but will embrace me with deep affection. Thank you, God. I pray in the precious name of Christ Jesus, my Lord and Savior. Amen.

The God who sent his only Son
to suffer and die for us will always
be with us in our sufferings.

$\mathcal{F}$or I consider that the sufferings of
this present time are not worthy
to be compared with the glory which
shall be revealed in us.

—Romans 8:18

CHAPTER 8

Experiencing Loneliness and Fears

To You I have cried out, O Lord,
And in the morning my prayer
comes before You . . . .
Loved one and friend You have
put far from me,
And my acquaintances into darkness.

—Psalm 88:13, 18

$\mathcal{O}$ Lord, this aloneness is almost more than I can take! If I could escape in a good night's sleep, I would. But my thoughts and fears and emotions are restless, hovering around this center of heartache. If it were not for you being here with me, I would despair. But your quiet presence keeps me from unraveling. These nights, these long drawn-out nights of solitude, are where I find you waiting, ready to speak comfort to my heart and assure me that you have a future in store for me that is good and worth waiting for. Tonight, even if sleep eludes me again, I'll continue to rest in your love for me.

If you look at the world, you'll be distressed.
If you look within, you'll be depressed.
If you look at God, you'll be at rest.

—Corrie ten Boom

Father, I don't want to give my fears power they don't deserve by brooding on them and imagining worst-case scenarios. Instead, I'll bring my concerns to you and tell you about them. I'll look at them in the light of your power, wisdom, and love. Then they will lose their hold over me as I trust in your goodness and rest in your providence. Thank you for showing me that this unbridled fear I sometimes allow to creep in leads to an unhealthy preoccupation with negative thoughts. I don't want to be a person who lives in fear and who incites others to be afraid. I want to be one who encourages and uplifts people, helping them see a hopeful reality.

Fear not, for I *am* with you;
Be not dismayed, for I *am* your God.
I will strengthen you,
Yes, I will help you,
I will uphold you with My
righteous right hand.

—Isaiah 41:10

When I feel like the people closest to me have let me down, Lord Jesus, help me remember that there have been times I've also failed others. I know it's okay for me to desire that truth, love, and faithfulness characterize my relationships, but you are the only one who has a perfect track record where those things are concerned. As a friend once told me, expectations are often little more than premeditated resentments. So, Lord, help me put my expectations and hopes where they belong: in your truth, love, and faithfulness. And help me be quick to extend the same forgiveness to others that you so readily extend to me when I let you down.

$\mathcal{M}$y relatives have failed,
And my close friends have forgotten me.

—Job 19:14

$\mathcal{J}$'ve been pondering this season of aloneness, Father. It's not something I would have chosen for myself, but you have chosen it for me in your great love for me. It's kind of like when an adolescent gets a practical gift from a parent, rather than toys or games or the childish gifts she had been used to receiving. At first there is a sort of letdown when the gift is opened, but later, when its usefulness is realized, there is a sense of appreciation and gratitude. That's what this solitude has become for me, dear Father. I am learning to delight in these times with you. I look forward to them more and more, and they are more nourishing spiritually and emotionally than all the socializing I used to arrange for myself. Thank you for this lovely gift of discovery!

If we are unwilling to pause and nurture our spiritual lives, sometimes God will bring it about in his own way, especially if we've asked him to help us grow spiritually.

𝓑e strong and of good courage,
do not fear nor be afraid of them;
for the Lord your God,
He *is* the One who goes with you.
He will not leave you nor forsake you.
—Deuteronomy 31:6

𝓘've been left all alone, and I feel so hurt and angry. Bitterness is trying to take root in my heart, Lord Jesus. Please help me! I know I need to reach a place of forgiveness, but right now, from where I'm standing, that looks like trying to leap across the Grand Canyon. I know you understand being abandoned. Your friends left you all alone during your hour of greatest need, and you knew they were going to do it. How did you still love them and wash their feet and speak kind words to them knowing what was coming? You leaned into the love of your Father, didn't you? Instead of focusing on who wasn't there for you, you focused on who was. Ah! That's my way over the canyon! Please heal my heart with your own love so I can be free to forgive.

*I*ndeed the hour is coming, yes,
has now come, that you will be scattered,
each to his own, and will leave Me alone.
And yet I am not alone, because
the Father is with Me.

—John 16:32

$\mathcal{I}$s there something new for me to learn in this imposed solitude, dear Lord? I know your Word says that there is a time and purpose for everything under heaven—even "a time to embrace and a time to refrain from embracing," according to the writer of Ecclesiastes. Well, Lord, I'm trying to trust that you have a purpose in this, but that purpose isn't clear to me, at least not yet. You know how much I am missing the "embrace" of human fellowship right now. Please let me sense the embrace of your fellowship more and more, not as a consolation prize but as the essence and source from which the best kind of fellowship can be had in this life. Help me be a good student, willing to learn as you work out your good purposes in my life.

Everything has its wonders, even darkness and silence, and I learn, whatever state I may be in, therein to be content.

—Helen Keller

Father, I don't want to be stuck anymore in this nexus of fear, of always trying to block every possible avenue of danger and mishap. It's too much work, and I need to learn to relax and trust you. Bad things could happen even if I take every precaution. And on the flip side, you are able to protect my life even in the most dangerous situation. I need to ask your forgiveness for trying to do your job, for trying to be my own ultimate protector. Teach me the difference, I pray, between being sensibly safe as I go along in life and being obsessed with precautionary measures at every turn. I feel a bit sheepish as I think how the people around me might feel grateful for this change in my life. Lord, it might help if you taught me to laugh a little at myself, too.

If I allow fear to dictate my actions/my next move, I will always be reacting to an imagined life rather than responding to my real one.

For God has not given us a spirit
of fear, but of power and of love
and of a sound mind.

—2 Timothy 1:7

$\mathcal{J}$'ve noticed, Lord, that when I push too much for someone to be my friend, my aspirations for friendship don't usually work out. I've also read that focusing too much on the goal of "getting" friends comes across as desperate and can sabotage a relationship. In this time of loneliness, dear Lord, I pray your Spirit would grant me patience and self-control, trusting that you will allow new friendships to unfold at the right time, in the right way. Help me be content in you and enjoy the people who come across my path, not worrying whether friendship will be the outcome.

*Just be friendly. Let the
"friend-chips" fall where they may.*

There is much more to this challenge of being alone than I might have imagined, Father. I would have thought boredom would have been the main issue with these fleeting feelings of loneliness. Not so! I'm finding that my mind is a veritable battlefield of thoughts. Self-pity; blaming you, myself, and others; defeatist attitudes; the temptation to seek out comfort in things I should not. Oh! The list is longer than that, but you know them all, Father. I need you to intervene, to check my thoughts with your truth. I know your Word is my best ally in keeping my thinking on track with what is right and true and good, so please help me keep the practice of reading your Word as a top priority now and always.

We have employments assigned to us for every circumstance in life. When we are alone, we have our thoughts to watch; in the family, our tempers; and in company, our tongues.
　　　　　　　　　　　　　　　—Hannah More

I'm tired of being afraid, Father! I want this to stop. That's why I'm stopping right here, right now to ask myself what it is I'm afraid of. Please, Father, I need your insight and courage to discover and face the true answer to that question. I want to look squarely at this and stop running from it. Help me find the freedom and healing you have for me, even if I need to seek counsel from an insightful friend or a professional. Here I am, Father. Let courage and faith see me through to the victory you hold out to me.

𝒯rust in Him at all times, you people;
Pour out your heart before Him;
God *is* a refuge for us.

—Psalm 62:8

*Fear is like radar that sees through the fog—
the reality of things at a distance that the
human eye cannot see.*

—Corrie ten Boom

You are opening my eyes, dear Lord, to the truth that my insecurities are a particularly destructive kind of fear in my life. Insecurity can cause me to miss out on adventure, new ideas, interesting people, opportunities for learning, and all sorts of life enrichment. The fear of trying something new, the fear of looking silly or feeling incompetent, the fear of someone else being better at something than I am—these are all unnecessary and limiting. I want to learn to be secure in your approval, Lord Jesus, to be set free in your love for me so that the prospect of stepping out into the unknown (and even possibly failing now and then) is a wonder-filled—not a fear-filled—thing.

Chip away at insecurities. Say hello to someone you don't know at church this week. Sign up for an interesting one-day seminar or class offered in your community. Write a letter to the editor regarding something you care about. Little victories build great courage.

The Lord is my rock and my fortress
and my deliverer;
My God, my strength, in whom
I will trust;
My shield and the horn of
my salvation, my stronghold.

—Psalm 18:2

I feel the danger of too much solitude, Father. The more I am alone, the more used to being alone I become. Usually I enjoy going to worship services, but I'm beginning to be tempted to just stay home and not go through the effort of getting myself up and ready to participate. I begin to think I can have as meaningful a service in my own home, listening to the worship music that resonates best with my spirit, reading your Word on my own, maybe listening to a Bible teacher on TV. But I know your Word clearly says that I should not "forsake the assembling" together with other believers. There is something to it, and as long as I am able to, I will follow your direction on this.

Believers are not compared to bears or lions
or other animals that wander alone.
Those who belong to Christ are sheep . . . .
Sheep go in flocks, and so do God's people.
—Charles Spurgeon

$\mathcal{J}$esus, scriptures say it is for freedom that you set us free. That sounds like a redundancy, but it's clear that you are trying to get a point across to us. Fear is not freedom, and your goal for us is freedom. Nothing less will do. I know I want to live in freedom, Lord, but sometimes the prospect of it scares me. Prison cells can seem safer than the big, wide world. They might be confining, but they're familiar. That's how I feel about my fear-based living sometimes: If I hold back or stay hidden, I feel safer. Oh, but how much I would miss of the joy and beauty and wonder of life! Set me free, then, Lord Jesus. Set me free!

*Christ is holding out his hand, ready
to lead us out of the prison of our fears.*

$\mathcal{N}$ow the Lord is the Spirit,
and where the Spirit of the Lord is,
there is freedom.

—2 Corinthians 3:17, NIV

$\mathcal{I}$ keep my eyes always on the Lord.
With him at my right hand,
I will not be shaken.

—Psalm 16:8, NIV

$\mathcal{J}$esus, what was it like when you felt abandoned
by your Father as you carried our sin for us?
Your Father was your closest companion. You
consulted him about everything. You were in
perfect communion with him. To feel forsaken
by him was certainly your darkest hour. When
I think of a worst fear for myself, it's probably
along the lines of rejection and abandonment.
Dear Jesus, you truly have tasted every type of
pain and sorrow, temptation and abuse known
to humankind. So it's to you, who has a truly
empathic heart, that I come for help in my time
of need. In my loneliness and fear, I ask you to be
my comfort and help today.

$\mathcal{J}$esus cried out with a loud voice,
saying, "Eli, Eli, lama sabachthani?"
that is, "My God, My God, why have
You forsaken Me?"
—Matthew 27:46

293

$\mathcal{P}$erfect love casts out fear. That's what I read in your Word, Lord. That statement keeps ringing in my ears. Does that mean your perfect love for me is able to demolish my fears, or does that mean as I truly learn to love and trust you there is no more room for fear in my life, only faith? Maybe the answer is both. I know your love for me is perfect; if I bring you my fears, you will deal with them as they deserve—out they go! But where there is still fear lingering in my heart, it's because I have yet to trust your love. I need to trust you enough to come to you and ask you to cast out these fears also. I ask, Lord, for that deeper trust.

God doesn't just politely usher fear
out of our lives: He casts it out.

$\mathcal{T}$hank you, Lord, for drawing me aside these days, away from the din of social life, to spend time with you. In this solitude, although it has been difficult at times, I have discovered spiritual strength in fellowship with you that I did not realize was possible. In this quietude, I can hear myself think and gather my thoughts and feelings to pray more meaningfully and sincerely. Instead of saying superficial (mostly self-serving) prayers on the fly as I rush around, I've been able to look more closely at essential things in my life. And what amazes me even more is that I can hear you speaking to me through your Word and encouraging me by your Spirit.

A soft and sheltered Christianity,
afraid to be lean and lone, unwilling to face
the storms and brave the heights,
will end up . . . in the cages of conformity.
— Vance Havner

When I'm by myself, all I need to do is remember you, dear Savior, and it makes all the difference! If I start focusing on how I wish it weren't so, or I brood about how someone left me out, or I fixate on how happy other people look together, I get sad and depressed, and things go from bad to worse. But if I choose, instead, to focus on you and think about who you are and how good you are to me, then I start to pray, thanking and praising you for all sorts of things. It starts turning into a personal worship service, and I end up encouraged rather than bummed out. Thank you for showing me that "alone" doesn't need to mean *lonely*.

The most lovely sort of fellowship is only a prayer away.

I will bless the Lord who
has given me counsel;
My heart also instructs me
in the night seasons.
—Psalm 16:7

*F*ather, my willpower is no match for resisting
the fears encroaching on my heart and mind.
I can resolve in the morning to not be afraid,
but unless I keep my eyes fixed steadily on you,
fear creeps in the door or blasts through my
resistances or catches me off guard. And you
know how easily distracted I become when the day
is underway. Oh, Father! I don't want to resist
my fears with mere willpower. Help me abandon
that strategy entirely and rely on you instead.
Remind me again and again that trusting you
means refusing to lean on my own understanding
and strength; I need to choose instead to lean on
yours. Amen.

It is madness to say, "I will not be afraid";
it is wisdom and peace to say,
"I will trust and not be afraid."

—Alexander MacLaren

$\mathcal{I}$ try to keep it out of my mind, Lord Jesus, but the older I get the more I encounter it. May I talk with you about the reality of death? I don't like to admit this, but even as one who trusts in you, I struggle not to fear death and dying. When I think of myself or ones I love entering "the valley of the shadow of death," I feel anxious and unsettled about the unknowns that surround it. It marks the end of life on earth. It separates. It bereaves. It does as it wishes, and we all must face it. But even now you console me. You understand. You tasted death, too. And even in that dark valley, you will walk alongside me. That is one thing I can be certain of.

Truly death delivers the most difficult and saddest of separations on earth, followed immediately by the most beautiful and joyous reunion imaginable in heaven.

*N*ow if we died with Christ, we believe
that we shall also live with Him.

—Romans 6:8

*J*esus, you were all alone in your commitment
to doing your Father's will. No one else on earth
has been so fully committed to obeying him
(without lapsing into selfishness at some point)
as you were. It must have been one long, lonely
road you walked here on earth. I recall that Isaiah
described you as a man of sorrows, familiar
with grief, despised, rejected. Jesus, that moves
me to think of you that way. It makes me realize
how much you identified with human suffering
while you walked among us. And how did you
get through it without giving up? The scriptures
reveal your secret: You spent lots of time alone
with your Father, praying, listening to him, being
instructed and encouraged. Thank you for your
example, Jesus. I will do the same today.

*N*ow in the morning, having risen
a long while before daylight, He went out
and departed to a solitary place;
and there He prayed.

—Mark 1:35

I've simply got to spend time talking with
you, Father. My heart is carrying more fear-
based cargo than it can hold. I need to bring
these things to you before I end up sinking my
ship in some kind of capsizing event I'll regret.
Please speak to calm the tumult in my heart right
now. And please, dear Father, don't let anything
interfere with this time I have with you. I'm going
to ignore distractions and talk to you about what's
going on. And in the talking, I know I will begin
trusting again. You are my safe harbor. You are
my place of refuge. I will always need you, Father.
Thank you for being here for me once again.

The ship of prayer may sail through
all temptations, doubts and fears, straight
up to the throne of God; and though she
may be outward bound with only griefs and
groans and sighs, she shall return freighted
with a wealth of blessings!

—Charles Spurgeon

*N*ow this is the confidence that
we have in Him, that if we ask anything
according to His will, He hears us.

—1 John 5:14

$\mathcal{I}$ just realized, Lord Jesus, how ironic it is that I've been aloof from you as I've been struggling with loneliness. I'm upset that others aren't here for me right now, while I'm turning my back on you. I know you don't get hurt and upset in the selfish ways I do, but still. It's quite an unkind thing to not value your love when you have loved me so well (and at such an unfathomable cost). I want to repent of my selfishness, not out of pity or pride but out of love. I do love you, Jesus, but I need you to help me mature in that love as I go along. Thank you for loving me as you do.

In our loneliness, when we neglect Jesus,
we are doing to him what we wish
others were not doing to us.

These times of fear and loneliness I've been going through, Lord, are becoming wells of experience from which I can draw empathy and encouragement to help others. The way I see it, this is another layer of redemption in my life. In my weakness and faithlessness, you lifted me up and taught me how to trust you. Now, all of that struggle and learning and growing is helping other people also learn and grow. It's a benefit I never thought to anticipate, and it brings me such joy to see you making these things all work together for good. I praise you for your grace and wisdom today, Jesus.

The Lord *is* good,
A stronghold in the day of trouble;
And He knows those who trust in Him.

—Nahum 1:7

You will have no test of faith that will not fit you to be a blessing if you are obedient to the Lord. I never had a trial but when I got out of the deep river I found some poor pilgrim on the bank that I was able to help by that very experience.

—A. B. Simpson

CHAPTER 9

Overcoming Anger and Cynicism

He who is slow to wrath
has great understanding.
—Proverbs 14:29

$\mathcal{D}$ear God, I'm so angry that I want to yell at somebody! Please stop me before I do. I know that once I let these words out of my mouth, I can't draw them back in, and I'll forever regret them. I confess I have a quick temper that at times is difficult for me to control. And so, I ask for your forgiveness. Let me not be swept up in this current cesspool of animosity and rancor. Help me not erupt in anger; let me always and immediately forgive and respond graciously, especially now, God, when my wrath is at its peak. Help me be your peacekeeper.

Let not your hand be raised in retaliation nor your voice in revenge.

For the wrath of man does not produce
the righteousness of God.

—James 1:20

The world is so corrupt and immoral, Lord, that it's hard not to be cynical. I see forces in the world spreading lies and deception. Some of these people even call themselves Christians, and their influence is widespread. I can't comprehend how grieved you must be, and yet you are still a loving and forgiving God. Lord, help me be like you, always ready to share the love of your Son with everyone. I want to be salt and not vinegar. I want to see your kingdom enlarged and not have a sour perspective toward others. I pray for this in the holy name of Jesus. Amen.

Cynicism makes things worse than they are in that it makes permanent the current condition, leaving us with no hope of transcending it.
—Richard Stivers

*D*ear Lord Jesus, please let my anger not turn into hate. I don't want to be known as a person of wrath; I would like to be identified as your follower, full of the fruit of the Spirit. I want to demonstrate peace, patience, kindness, and goodness. But it's hard! I have so much rage boiling inside of me because of what was done to me and what was said about me. How can they be so vindictive? I did nothing to deserve their abuse. I know, Jesus, I need to switch my focus from them to you. I need to see how much you've forgiven me so I can forgive. I also need to see their need for you. And so, Lord, I pray for them and for me—that we all will come under your guiding hand.

Jesus did not show anger toward those who abused him but demonstrated anger toward those who abused the less fortunate.

*D*o not take revenge, my dear friends,
but leave room for God's wrath;
for it is written, "It is mine to avenge;
I will repay," says the Lord.

—Romans 12:19, NIV

$\mathcal{A}$lmighty God, there are enough cynics in the world without me being one of them. But with so much suffering and injustice in the world, it's hard not to fall into despair. How can people be so cruel to each other? Both governments and individuals commit unspeakable atrocities— it's so unbelievable! Instead of wallowing in gloom, however, I want to do something that will somehow ease the suffering of others. I want to be a positive force in the world. And I know I can only do this if I first let Jesus rule my life and show me what I can and should do. So help me, God, to change my cynical attitude and be more Christlike when I approach the world.

Jesus was never cynical;
cynicism is the worst enemy of joy.

Out of the depths I have cried to You,
O Lord; Lord, hear my voice!
Let Your ears be attentive
To the voice of my supplications.
—Psalm 130:1–2

I need to be angry, Lord; this sinful behavior is wrong. But I have to be careful how I talk to this person who is committing these acts of rebellion. I don't want to alienate them. And so, Lord, I need you to help me control my anger. Teach me to be both wise and merciful in my anger, so that this person will have the opportunity to repent and turn to you for guidance. I want to be severe and just. I want this person to come to your grace but only on your terms. And if this person still refuses to turn away from sin, help me continue to love and pray for this person but never to lessen my disdain for and anger against sin.

A man that does not know how to be angry
does not know how to be good.
Now and then a man should be shaken
to the core with indignation over things evil.
—Henry Ward Beecher

317

So then, my beloved brethren,
let every man be swift to hear,
slow to speak, slow to wrath.

—James 1:19

*H*oly God, you know that I wasn't always cynical. But the hardships of life have just worn me down. Time after time either circumstances or a person's actions have knocked me down, and now I just don't want to get up anymore. Why should I? I'll just be knocked down again. Each time a little more hope seeps out of me. Now there's nothing left. I look back, and I see myself when I was so much younger and had such an optimistic view of life. Not anymore! Life is just too tough. But, God, I'm so wretched. Tear down my cynicism. Fill me with hope and a renewed vision for my life. Please give me meaning. I want to feel significant again. Please help me, God.

When a person cries out to God,
there's still hope in that person.

$\mathcal{I}$ don't want to rush to anger, heavenly Father. It's what everyone expects me to do—and perhaps, some want me to do. But I don't want anger to be lodged in my heart, settling in and taking possession of me. If I'm to be angry, I want to come to it slowly and deliberately so I can speak and behave in the way you wish. So take control of my emotions, Father, and guide me through this volatile situation. You know best how I should channel my anger while displaying my faith in Christ. I live to please you and not my feelings for others. Thank you for being my caring Father.

$\mathcal{D}$o not hasten in your spirit to be angry,
For anger rests in the bosom of fools.

—Ecclesiastes 7:9

$\mathcal{L}$ord Jesus, help me resist the strong tide of
cynicism that is sweeping across our society.
It's easy to see why people have become cynical,
but I don't want to be that way. I don't want
to be a grumbler; I want to be an encourager.
I don't want to be stuck in the quicksand of
disappointment; I want to step forward full of
your joy and hope. When I get cynical, Lord
Jesus, remind me that you're in control of my

life and human history and that our destiny is wondrously secure. I praise you, Jesus, for you're greater than anything in this world, and I'm glad that I can always look to you to see the bright side of life.

The light of God's Son shines brighter than any star in the heavens.

The Lord *is* my strength and my shield;
My heart trusted in Him, and I am helped;
Therefore my heart greatly rejoices,
And with my song I will praise Him.

—Psalm 28:7

I confess, almighty God, that I sometimes enjoy being angry. It's exhilarating, and I love to feed it with vengeful thoughts. When someone gets my goat, I fantasize about the many ways I can get back at that person. I know it's an ugly part of me. I know it's wrong to dwell on my anger in the way that I do. Most of all, I know I need your help to stop being vindictive and to be pure in my heart and my mind. So, God, I come to you now because anger is again stirring within me, and I need you to rule over my thoughts. Thank you, God, for taking over me.

Anger is short-lived in a good man.
—Thomas Fuller

Lord, when I really consider the things I am cynical about, I realize how Satan has sidetracked me from the things you want me to focus on. It is an attack on my faith, and in reality, cynicism is a sign of my doubt in your omnipotence and holiness. I see that clearly now. Oh Lord, please pull me out of the alluring clutches of cynicism. Help me not to be bitter and irritable. I want to be your ambassador of good news about Jesus. I want to talk about the things that are important to you and not things that are only important to me. Actually, Lord, I want those things that are important to you to be important to me. I pray in the precious name of your Son, Jesus. Amen.

If we are to be God's salt in this world, we must rid ourselves of all forms of cynicism.

*L*et all bitterness, wrath, anger, clamor, and evil speaking be put away from you, with all malice. And be kind to one another, tenderhearted, forgiving one another, even as God in Christ forgave you.

—Ephesians 4:31–32

$\mathscr{I}$ don't want to be a wrathful person, heavenly Father. I want to be a person you delight in, but it's not easy to be the person you want me to be because of the circumstances I'm currently in. There are those who are constantly nasty to me, and I can only take so many of their vile attacks. And yet, I know whatever I can't take, you will take for me, if I would only rest in your Spirit and trust in your Word. Through scripture, you promise that you will always provide a way of escape from any situation that threatens my faith in you. Help me, Father, for I'm in that situation now. Help me be the person you want me to be.

We are being molded into the image of Christ
as long as we remain in the hands of God.

The discretion of a man makes him
slow to anger, And his glory *is* to
overlook a transgression.

—Proverbs 19:11

Lord, it's not difficult for me to believe in
you. The real challenge for me is in believing
some of your promises, particularly the promise
to transform us in the image of Christ. I see
how some Christians behave and hear their
attitudes, and I wonder whether your Spirit is
actually changing them into better people. I
can understand a new believer having a load of

327

worldly baggage, but believers who have attended church and worshiped you for many years? They still seem self-centered and judgmental and full of greed and gossip. I don't understand. Help me, Lord, not to doubt your wisdom. Instead, help me to trust your Word and rely on it more faithfully. And help me to attend to my own commitment to be more like Jesus. Maybe I need to look at myself in the same way I'm viewing others. Please help me align my vision to yours.

The issue of faith is not so much whether we believe in God, but whether we believe the God we believe in.

—R. C. Sproul

$\mathcal{I}$'m angry, Jesus, not for myself but for my loved one who was treated so unfairly. I want to tell off those responsible for my loved one's tears. How could they be so cruel? They deserve to be severely reprimanded, but I suppose not by me. I would be overly harsh and unreasonable. Instead of lashing out in anger against them, please turn my attention to my loved one, providing support and encouragement. Help me, Jesus, to be sensitive and insightful. Let me be your vessel of love. And thank you, Jesus, for caring for my loved one through me and for curbing my anger as well. I can't do what you are calling me to do without your gentleness and kindness.

Caring for others shall be the touchstone
of our faith in Jesus Christ.

*L*et all *that* you *do* be done with love.

—1 Corinthians 16:14

Wherever I go, God, I am met with so much cynicism against Christians. Today, it's not cool to be a faithful Christian in many places in our society. I suppose to a certain extent, we demonstrate our failings too clearly to the world, but I think many accusations are far too critical and off base. Listening or reading their statements often makes me cynical—not about my brothers and sisters in Christ but about nonbelievers. I'm aghast at their false portrayals of us, and especially you, but I'm even more aghast at my own reactions when you place a mirror in front of me. I believe you love them. Help me, God, to overcome my cynicism and love them as you do. Help me be to them as you are to me—patient and oh so gracious!

But I say to you who hear: Love your enemies, do good to those who hate you, bless those who curse you, and pray for those who spitefully use you.

—Luke 6:27–28

Almighty God, you know how easily I say hurtful words when I lose my cool. You know that I've lost several friends because of my unbridled tongue and easily provoked pride. I don't have the humility to confess my faults to others and ask them for forgiveness; my pride is simply too stubborn. I even find it difficult to make this confession to you, but I'm so desperate for your help. I can't change on my own. I need you to change me. So, God, please teach me the humility and gentleness I find in Christ. Help me to be like your Son. I pray in his holy name. Amen.

The designs of our heart must be drawn by our Lord God if we are to be pure in spirit.

$\mathcal{B}$y nature, Lord, I'm a cynical person. I tend to see the glass half empty on most matters. Whenever I see a cloud, I think it's going to be stormy. Whenever I hear a bird sing, I look to see where they made a mess. Whenever someone gives me a compliment, I wonder what's the ulterior motive. Although you often bless me, I'm always counting the cost of being your disciple. My attitude is insane! I should be full of joy for all that you've done for me. Forgive me, Lord! For surely my cup runs over from all that you've given me. Though I'm certainly unworthy of your love, I'm truly grateful for your favor.

The cost of being Christ's disciple is not a burden but a blessing to be praised.

Then Jesus spoke to them again, saying, "I am the light of the world. He who follows Me shall not walk in darkness, but have the light of life."

—John 8:12

God, I was right to say what I said, but I was wrong in the way I said it. I couldn't help but express myself in anger, an anger that kept growing as I kept speaking. And then I realized—I wasn't being heard. Instead, I was inflaming the people I spoke to. Anger was spreading from me to them. It became an uncontrollable wildfire. My righteous anger wasn't righteous at all. I blew it, God. Please forgive me. I want to serve you effectively, and in order to do that, I must let you control my anger. Help me, God!

No matter how just your words may be, you ruin everything when you speak with anger.

—John Chrysostom

Because people have burned me so many times in the past, heavenly Father, I now distrust everyone. Not only do I disbelieve the sincerity of people's motives for what they do and say, but I also scorn those who show me any type of friendly behavior. As a result, my cynicism has secluded me from almost all social interaction. It's a terrible way to live, Father, especially for a Christian like me. I know I need to break out of my self-imposed shell, not only to be in regular fellowship with other believers but also to pursue relationships with nonbelievers. I'm sorry that I've become like this. Please, Father, open my heart once again so I can be a true servant of Christ, not only for his sake but for my sake as well. I pray in Jesus' holy name. Amen.

And whatever you do in word or deed,
do all in the name of the Lord Jesus, giving
thanks to God the Father through Him.
—Colossians 3:17

*Without being a doormat that people walk on,
as followers of Christ, we must always have
a forgiving and open heart.*

$\mathcal{D}$ear Lord Jesus, how can I stop from being so angry? I don't want that anger to turn into hatred. I don't want to become so wrathful that I cause lasting harm to those with whom I'm angry. When I get this upset, it absorbs my entire being. My emotions become so intensely fierce that I can't function normally. Instead, I continuously dwell on what stirred my anger and what I want to do about it. Dear Jesus, stop me now! Help me put away my anger and be obedient to your teachings. Help me turn my other cheek and pray for those who've hurt me. I so want to be like you.

*B*ut I tell you not to resist an evil
person. But whoever slaps you on your
right cheek, turn the other to him also.

—Matthew 5:39

*T*oday, Lord, I'm really cynical. I don't know
why I feel like this. It's just like any other day.
Nothing is different about me or my life. The
world seems the same today as it was yesterday. I
don't know if what's wrong with me is biological
or something else. I only know that I feel very
gloomy and pessimistic. Life is simply a drag.
Lord, please deliver me out of my wretched
doldrums. Please fill my heart with your joy and
my mind with thoughts on how I can serve you
today. I praise you, Lord, for being so powerful
and so caring that you can and will encourage me
to be the child you want me to be.

*Mighty is our Lord God
and greatly to be praised.*

I know, God, that there's nothing wrong with anger visiting me now and then. Even Jesus was angry at times, such as when he chased the moneychangers from the temple in Jerusalem. And you were also angry with your people, the ancient Hebrews, whenever they rebelled against you. But I also know that you don't want anger to take up residence in our souls. So when it's appropriate, God, please help me get rid of my anger. I don't want it to be my constant companion; I want Jesus to be that. Teach me to be like your Son in every way. I pray in his holy name. Amen.

He who is slow to anger *is* better than
the mighty, And he who rules his spirit
than he who takes a city.

—Proverbs 16:32

$\mathscr{F}$or to this you were called,
because Christ also suffered for us,
leaving us an example,
that you should follow His steps.

—1 Peter 2:21

*L*ord God, some people say that I'm too critical.
I don't think that I am. I think I'm being realistic
about life and people. I'm a pragmatic person,
and I don't look at things with a Pollyanna
attitude. But, Lord, if people say that I'm overly
harsh in my judgments, then there must be
something in me that leaves those impressions.
So, please show me how I need to correct this
part of myself. I don't want my witness for Jesus
to tarnish his image to others. I want you to be
pleased with my service to Christ in this world. So
help me, Lord, to adjust my attitude so it reflects
your love, not my judgment.

*Every follower of Christ has a God-given
ministry in this world, and therefore,
we are all divinely responsible for how we
behave and what we say to others.*

*L*et no corrupt word proceed out
of your mouth, but what is good for
necessary edification, that it may
impart grace to the hearers.

—Ephesians 4:29

I confess, heavenly Father, I'm enraged by what
just occurred. The situation became so volatile
that I stormed out before I said something I knew
I would regret. Father, please calm me down.
Please place your hand on me and keep me from
letting loose my boiling anger. I'm seething with
outrage over what was said about me. It's gross
slander! Oh Father, you can see how much this
has upset me. I need to find refuge in your love
in order for my anger to dissipate. I need you so
badly. Please comfort me! I pray in the precious
name of Jesus. Amen.

*Let us bow our knees before our Lord Jesus,
and thank him for his gracious love
and his glorious presence.*

"Be angry, and do not sin": do not let
the sun go down on your wrath.

—Ephesians 4:26

CHAPTER 10

Hurting in a Relationship

For the eyes of the Lord *are* on the righteous, And His ears *are open* to their prayers. . . . And who *is* he who will harm you if you become followers of what is good? But even if you should suffer for righteousness' sake, *you are* blessed.

—1 Peter 3:12–14

Father, I don't understand why this relationship has suddenly deteriorated. If there is something I've done, something I need to make right, please show me, and I'll make amends. But you know I haven't done anything intentional. Right now I'm reeling and want to lash out, but I need you to keep me from doing that. When this initial pain lessens, help me rid my thoughts of bitterness and revenge. Even though I feel I've been wronged, I don't want to add another wrong to the situation. I'll leave justice in your hands. Help me focus now on "keeping my side of the street clean" and responding in ways that honor you and are in keeping with my desire to walk before you in truth and love.

A good man is kinder to his enemy
than bad men to their friends.

—Joseph Hall

*T*herefore, as *the* elect of God,
holy and beloved, put on tender mercies,
kindness, humility, meekness,
long-suffering; bearing with one another,
and forgiving one another, if anyone has a
complaint against another; even as Christ
forgave you, so you also *must do.*

—Colossians 3:12–13

$\mathcal{R}$ight now, I'm struggling with self-complacency, Lord Jesus. You see the thoughts running through my head: *I* could never do *that* to a friend! Have I failed my friends in ways that might cause them to think that of me? I know I need to extend grace and forgiveness in this situation. It's what I would desire from my friend if the tables were turned. This thing in me that wants to inflict punishment—to act hurt and angry, to withdraw my goodwill, to impose a silent treatment—I need your Spirit to help me resist it. This failure doesn't characterize my friend, and I know I shouldn't behave as though it does. I want to be like you and extend forgiveness in such a way that we can soon move on as if this never happened.

No man can expect to find a friend
without faults, nor can he propose
himself to be so to another.
—Owen Feltham

$\mathcal{P}$lease help me, Lord Jesus! I'm devastated by what has happened and don't know how to go forward. Maybe I gave this relationship too much importance in my life. Lord, I'm afraid I've even put it ahead of my relationship with you at times. I've been wrong to do that. It's so clear now: this person I elevated to such a high place in my world is gone, but you are still here with me. As I turn to you now in my pain and sorrow, you could hold my wrong priorities against me, but you respond to me with compassion and kindness. Thank you for being the truest of friends.

The dearest friend on earth is a
mere shadow compared to Jesus Christ.
—Oswald Chambers

For *it is* not an enemy *who*
reproaches me;
Then I could bear *it*.
Nor *is it* one *who* hates me who has
exalted *himself* against me;
Then I could hide from him.
But *it was* you, a man my equal,
My companion and my acquaintance.
We took sweet counsel together,
And walked to the house of God
in the throng.

—Psalm 55:12–14

This hostility toward me, Lord, shakes me to the core. I understand disagreement and conflict and working through differences, but I don't understand hatred. At first, when the daggers of spite and malice fly at me, I feel frightened. Then a self-preserving anger rises up in me. I don't want to be cruel, but I do want to set the record straight and tell the other person they're out of line. How do I keep my integrity in these situations, Father? The treatment I'm receiving amounts to abuse, and I know it's wrong. I feel compelled to confront it, but I lack courage and wisdom to know when and how. In the end, I pray that you would help me act prudently and that you would restore a culture of kindness and safety around me.

*If hostility passes through my camp,
that is one thing. But if it puts down stakes
in my camp, I must either exercise my
right to move away from it or accept my
responsibility to address it.*

*E*ven my own familiar friend
in whom I trusted,
Who ate my bread,
Has lifted up *his* heel against me.

—Psalm 41:9

*W*e've had a falling out, Father. My friend
and I are at odds, and I am frustrated with how
unreasonable things have become. I know I need
to own my part in what has transpired, but my
pride is getting in the way. What if I'm the only
one to apologize, especially when I feel I have the
smaller part to confess in what went wrong? What
if things are never truly addressed or forgiven
on both sides? I don't want there to be a rift, but
I also don't want to move forward under false
pretenses. I need your wisdom, Father. That's why
I'm here. Help me put my pride aside and listen
to your heart in this matter.

What a friend we have in Jesus,
all our sins and griefs to bear!
What a privilege to carry
everything to God in prayer! . . .
Do thy friends despise, forsake thee?
Take it to the Lord in prayer!
In his arms he'll take and shield thee;
Thou wilt find a solace there.

—Joseph M. Scriven

*Friendships must be carefully selected,
lovingly sustained, and prayerfully upheld.*

$\mathcal{L}$ord, I've learned that some people I considered friends have been gossiping about me. What's worse, the rumors are false and slanderous. These aren't my closest friends, but it still hurts. What am I supposed to do now? Avoid them? Be polite but distant? Forgive them? Even if I forgive them, Lord, which I know I must do, they've broken my trust. I guess the bottom line is that if my relationships with these people still matter to me, I need to let them know that they've hurt me. Then, if our friendship matters to them, they'll acknowledge what they've done, apologize, and we can move on from there. Please guide me through this mess, and help me do what's best.

All relationships require nurture.
The closer the relationship,
the more nurturing it will need.

$\mathcal{A}$t one time, I imagined that marriage would be a wonderful friendship, a fairy tale of ongoing love and support. Now I know, marriage is a lot of work! It's two people, with two separate backgrounds and sets of ideas and ways of doing things—especially ways of relating—trying to find a way to live and work together! And in all honesty, Lord, it's painful a lot of the time. After a long while of struggling, a level of indifference can set in, and one or both of us takes the other for granted. Lord, I want my marriage to grow, not die. Right now, I feel like it's in jeopardy. Please help! Guide us back to ways of relating to each other with meaningful love and respect.

$\mathcal{H}$atred stirs up strife,
But love covers all sins.
—Proverbs 10:12

$\mathcal{F}$ather, your Word reveals that your Son was betrayed with a kiss—a false greeting arranged by a treacherous friend. What terrible hypocrisy! I cannot relate to betrayal on that level, but what has been done to me was treacherous and false. You know how it blindsided me. I am hurt and angry and humiliated. I keep thinking of ways to retaliate, but I can't let those thoughts go too far without remembering how Jesus responded to his ordeal. From the moment he was betrayed, until the moment he died, he continued to entrust himself to you, knowing you would vindicate him at the right time. And at the resurrection, you did just that! So, while this betrayal doesn't even begin to compare, I know that you can help me as I walk through this pain.

*J*esus said to him, "Judas, are you betraying the Son of Man with a kiss?"
—Luke 22:48

$\mathcal{D}$ear Jesus, how faithful you were in your friendships and how faithless your friends were in return. Knowing their fears and weaknesses, you extended forgiveness when they failed, and you did not give up on them; you knew their faith was not fully grown. Help me be patient in my relationships, too, especially when my friends and family fail to meet my expectations or fulfill my desires for what I feel a good friend should be. If I'm going to grow to be more like Christ, I need to be willing to see relationships through, even when these people I love let me down from time to time. And, dear Lord, help me see where I have failed my friends. Teach me to be a good friend, so I can teach my friends.

If thou art willing to suffer no adversity,
how wilt thou be the friend of Christ?
—Thomas à Kempis

As I've been going through this trial, Lord, I feel as if my friends have scattered. At first, when things were difficult for me, they were supportive. But now that this ordeal has continued, I don't hear from anyone, and no one accepts my invitations to visit. I feel excluded, and it hurts. Are they afraid of saying the wrong thing? Is it that they don't know how to respond to me? Is my situation too "messy" for them? Are they afraid that's all I'm going to want to talk about? I long to go back to old times when things were normal, but that isn't possible. Lord, I place my desire for fellowship in your hands.

The lonely miles of my journey are miles that can teach me to recognize the look of another lonely soul who could use encouragement.

*C*ommit your way to the Lord,
Trust also in Him,
And He shall bring *it* to pass.
—Psalm 37:5

*L*ord, you see how my friend has become my
enemy, and you know I long to find a way to
heal the relationship. I feel misunderstood
and misjudged, but I haven't been given the
opportunity to set the record straight. In the
meantime, my friend is reacting out of hurt and
anger, saying and doing things that are hard to
take. And not only are her words and attitude

hurtful, but it's painful to know she believes something so awful about me. Oh, Lord, help me show her love despite all of this anger, and please let love open the door for reconciliation. But if she continues to consider me her enemy, by your grace, let your love flow through me and toward her still.

If your enemy is hungry,
give him bread to eat;
And if he is thirsty,
give him water to drink. . .
And the Lord will reward you.
—Proverbs 25:21–22

$\mathscr{I}$ so want to find a way to have a relationship with this person in my family, Lord, although you see their way of approaching a relationship is highly dysfunctional. I cannot help loving this person you've put in my life. I just don't know how to navigate being around them when their hurts, habits, and hang-ups are constantly wreaking havoc. Do I stay away? Do I press in? Do I confront? Do I just pray and show kindness? I don't know what is best, but I know you do. Please grant me wisdom; help me listen to your guidance and follow through, even if it's difficult to accept.

The most difficult relationships are those we wait for, never knowing if they will be made whole, yet always hoping, because love tethers our hearts there.

*L*ove suffers long *and* is kind; love does
not envy; love does not parade itself, is
not puffed up; does not behave rudely,
does not seek its own, is not provoked,
thinks no evil; does not rejoice in
iniquity, but rejoices in the truth;
bears all things, believes all things,
hopes all things, endures all things.

—1 Corinthians 13:4–7

*S*ometimes people are so frustrating, Father!
You see our opposing viewpoints—my friend's
and mine—and how divisive our perspectives
become at times when we throw kindness out the
window in the heat of conversation. I know that
differences are bound to happen in a friendship,
but this last argument felt like the end when we
walked away. Father, help me! I know you are
reminding me that a bit of humility goes a long
way in restoring things. I can approach him and
apologize for my bad attitude, and then hopefully
he'll be able to see how our willingness to agree

to disagree has always held up over time . . . that is, when we've made love and respect our first priority. Please keep our hearts open to this friendship. I would miss him very much if he weren't in my life.

A quarrel between friends, when made up,
adds a new tie to friendship.
Be who you are, and be that well.
—St. Francis de Sales

$\mathcal{L}$isten to your father who begot you,
And do not despise your mother
when she is old.

—Proverbs 23:22

$\mathcal{A}$s my parent gets older, heavenly Father,
it's becoming more challenging to know my
responsibilities. It's as if our roles are reversing,
and yet, neither of us really feels comfortable
with the change. How do I honor the dignity of
this person who has reared me, even as I have to
establish rules for the sake of my parent's safety
and well-being? How do I know when to step
in and when to leave things as they are? It's so
difficult! I don't want to make a mistake. I don't
want to cause any harm by neglect, nor do I
want to impose. I need your insight and wisdom
to walk down this path. Please grant both of
us sufficient patience and grace to accept each
change along the way.

*Caring for an aging parent is a
once-in-a-lifetime opportunity to say
thank you, to give back, to remember,
to forgive, to heal, to understand,
to bless, to love finally and fully.*

It's less the words they say than those they leave unsaid that split old friends apart.

—Frederick Beuchner

*F*ather, I've felt distance growing between us—my friend and me. Some unresolved hurts have been allowed to linger, and that poison has infiltrated our relationship. We've both tried pretending everything's okay, but we both know it's not. I guess it feels embarrassing to talk about offenses that seem childish but truly hurt our hearts. I'm not sure where to begin or how to approach her. Please open a door of opportunity for us to speak truthfully to one another so we can deal with this issue once and for all. I know that's what you would have us do.

Say to those *who are* fearful-hearted,
"Be strong, do not fear!
Behold, your God will
come *with* vengeance,
With the recompense of God;
He will come and save you."

—Isaiah 35:4

Father, it is becoming increasingly clear to
me that hurts from my past are still affecting
my relationships today. I am beginning to see
how I bring my insecurities and fears into my
new relationships and hold others hostage with
them, continually requiring people to prove
their friendship to me. This need I have to be
reassured is driving away the people I most want a
relationship with. Dear Father, I need your help
in finding healing from these fears. I need to find
my sense of security in your love for me so that
I'm not putting the responsibility on others to
make me feel secure. Restore my soul, and help
me stop looking to others for what only you can
supply. I pray this in your Son's name.

When we look to others for what only Christ can give, we will never fail to be disappointed. Our sense of happiness, contentment, and security must be found in him alone.

My children are beginning to see me less as their "hero," Lord, and more as "just human." It's hard to lose that place in their hearts and minds. They're seeing that I don't have all the answers, that I fail at different times and in different ways. They're seeing my frailty and weakness, and I've lost esteem in their eyes. Help me be patient with my children as they come to terms with these realizations. Help me remember that it's part of the process they must go through as they move toward becoming independent, mature adults. Mend their hurts and disappointments, Father, and cause our relationship to grow in depth and dimension as time goes on. Thank you for these children you've given me. I love them so!

There is no friendship, no love,
like that of the parent for the child.
—Henry Ward Beecher

For great is your love toward me;
you have delivered me from the depths.
—Psalm 86:13, NIV

This is perhaps the most difficult relational decision I've ever had to make, Lord. I'm anxious and relieved to be stepping out of this relationship with the person I've been praying to you so much about. You know I didn't really want to come to this conclusion, that I've been denying just how toxic this individual's attitudes, perspectives, words, and actions are. I've made excuses and rationalizations and have downplayed the impact of the negativity. But, Lord, I see how it's affecting others around me, and it's time for me to stand up for what is right and good and true. Conversations have not helped, so please help me now as I take meaningful action. I truly hope this person will choose to make some meaningful changes, but in the meantime, thank you for leading me to safety.

When moving away from someone is the best course of action for our well-being, continued prayer for that person is a way to keep on loving them from a distance.

Lord Jesus, I sincerely want to be more like you in my relationships, even in the ones that are unpleasant and difficult right now. I want the relationships in my life to have more depth, to be richer and more meaningful as I love more authentically and intentionally. Even if my love is not reciprocated, Lord, even if some of the people in my life do not know how to love, I know that by choosing to love them anyway, I will grow to understand more of what it means to love like you do. Today I choose—no matter what—to love the people you've placed in my life.

$\mathcal{L}$ove as brothers,
be tenderhearted, *be* courteous;
not returning evil for evil or reviling
for reviling, but on the contrary blessing,
knowing that you were called to this,
that you may inherit a blessing.

—1 Peter 3:8–9

$\mathcal{Y}$ou know I'm not always good at receiving criticism, Father, not even the constructive kind. Psalm 141 says, "Let the righteous strike me; *It shall* be a kindness. And let him rebuke me; *It shall* be as excellent oil; Let my head not refuse it." That's such a noble way to think and act, and I want to be that kind of person, but whenever my friend gives me negative feedback, I get so defensive and feel hurt. I need to grow in this area, Lord. I want to be able to see my friend's input as a kindness. Please help me move past my insecurity and see the blessing in having a friend who loves me enough to tell me difficult things.

*He is your friend who pushes
you nearer to God.*
—Abraham Kuyper

An emotionally needy person is pursuing a friendship with me, Lord. I don't want to turn him away, but I know I cannot give him the amount of time and attention he wants. Part of me wants to run away from his demands, and the other part of me wants to stay and give him what I am able and willing to give in the way of fellowship. Please give me the compassion to care and still keep boundaries the relationship needs to remain healthy, for his sake and for mine. Please give me strength to stick to the parameters you are helping me set, and help me demonstrate your genuine love within those boundaries. It's not my pity he needs, Lord; it's love—your love.

*A*s water reflects the face,
so one's life reflects the heart.
—Proverbs 27:19, NIV

*The love of God motivates us to love others
whenever we ask ourselves, "Where would I
be today if someone hadn't shown me
what God's love is like?"*

*N*ow may the God of patience and comfort
grant you to be like-minded toward one
another, according to Christ Jesus, that you
may with one mind and one mouth glorify
the God and Father of our Lord Jesus Christ.

—Romans 15:5-6

$\mathcal{B}$e of good comfort, be of one mind,
live in peace; and the God of love and
peace will be with you.

—2 Corinthians 13:11

Acknowledgments

Photo Credits